HOLLISA ALEWINE

STANDING
WITH
ISRAEL

A HOUSE OF PRAYER
FOR ALL NATIONS

ACW
PRESS

ACW Press
Ozark, AL 36360

STANDING WITH ISRAEL: A House of Prayer for All Nations
Copyright ©2005 Hollisa Alewine
All rights reserved

Cover Design by Alpha Advertising
Interior Design by Pine Hill Graphics

Packaged by ACW Press
1200 HWY 231 South #273
Ozark, AL 36360
www.acwpress.com
The views expressed or implied in this work do not necessarily reflect those of ACW Press. Ultimate design, content, and editorial accuracy of this work is the responsibility of the author(s).

Library of Congress Cataloging-in-Publication Data
(Provided by Cassidy Cataloguing Services, Inc.)
Alewine, Hollisa.

   Standing with Israel : a house of prayer for all nations / Hollisa
   Alewine. -- 1st ed. -- Ozark, AL : ACW Press, 2005.

      p. ; cm.
      ISBN: 1-932124-51-9

      1. Messianic Judaism. 2. Jewish messianic movements.
   3. Prayer--Judaism. 4. Prayer. 5. Fellowship--Religious aspects.
   I. Title.

BM615 .A44 2005
289.9--dc22   0502

Printed in the United States of America.

For Mom

For we know that if the earthly tent which is our house is torn down, we have a building from God, a house not made with hands, eternal in the heavens.

CONTENTS

FOREWORD

Christians today often struggle with the same questions about the Holy Land that have plagued hundreds of generations before us. Should Christians support Israel in the face of growing negative world opinion? How much of what we see and read in the media concerning the historical and political problems between Israel and the Arabs and Palestinians is factual? Are the Jews of Israel the "older brother" of the Judeo-Christian heritage and deserving of Christian loyalty? Where do Christians fit in the covenant picture? Are they part of Israel? Have they replaced Israel? Are there really two separate covenants? The aim of *Standing With Israel* is not to present easy answers to these questions. If there are answers to the political, economic, military, theological, and historical questions, it is the reader who will have to investigate them. For those so motivated, there is a resource page included with the glossary. No matter what the questions are, it is the aim of *Standing With Israel* to reply to all of them with one answer: prayer.

Non-Jews in Scripture enter into proper relationship with Jews in two ways. One way is through loyal service and kindness to the Jews. The loyal service and kindness are illustrated by Ruth, Rahab, and two Roman officers. The other method of entering a proper Biblical relationship with the Jews is prayerful earnest petition, illustrated by the Syro-Phoenician woman and Cornelius. The Scriptural examples establish the pattern for any future first steps in relations between Jews and non-Jews: acts of kindness and prayer.

7

While political or military alliances may have their places in the kingdoms of men, it is the alliance of prayer that advances the Kingdom of Heaven. *Standing With Israel* teaches the non-Jew about Jewish prayer, and should the reader accept the invitation, teaches the non-Jew how to pray the Jewish prayer, the same Three O'Clock Prayer that Cornelius prayed.

Prayer for the Jew has changed little since the days of Ezra and Nehemiah. The basic framework of the prayer prayed three times daily by observant Jews is the Amidah, which means "Standing." Therefore, if one stands with the Jews, he prays with the Jews. *Standing With Israel* is no less than praying the Standing Prayer, the Amidah. This prayer is composed of eighteen individual benedictions, and so the prayer is also nicknamed Eighteen, or Shemoneh Esrei in Hebrew.

There are other Hebrew terms in *Standing With Israel* that non-Jews may not know, but are important in retaining the cultural heritage of the prayer. The Bible that Jesus used was written in Hebrew and Aramaic. Jesus was a Jew from the tribe of Judah, and He spoke and read fluent Hebrew and Aramaic. His Name is *Yeshua*, and it means "Salvation" in Hebrew. The Bible that Jesus used was the ancient Jewish division of Scriptures called the *Torah* (Law), Prophets, and the Writings, which includes Psalms. The Hebrew acronym for this is the *Tanakh*, or what Christians call The Old Testament. The author will often use Torah, which means God's teaching and instruction, to refer to the Scriptures. Because of their reverence for the most holy Name of God, most Jews substitute *Hashem* (the Name) or *Adonai* (Lord) in order to keep from profaning the Sacred Name that is often mistranslated and mispronounced in English Bibles as Jehovah, which is not nor has ever been a Hebrew word. The Holy Spirit is the *Ruach HaKodesh*. A glossary is provided to aid the reader with no background in Hebrew.

When Christians think of Jews praying, they may envision swaying, long-bearded and black-garbed men draped in large woolen prayer shawls and wearing little black leather boxes strapped to forehead and forearm. That image may stir feelings of curiosity. It may arouse a deep spiritual identification with the Covenant People. One may be envious of the ancient heritage or thankful that he or she does not have to participate in such old ritual prayer. Learning a few things about Jewish prayer equips the Christian with knowledge to establish a lasting bond with his Jewish brothers in the timeless realm of prayer and removes some of the mystery.

If the reader would stand with Israel, let us find a common language of prayer, then pray with sincerity the opening line of the Amidah, "My Adonai, open my lips that my mouth may declare Your praise!"

PART 1

*Historic and Prophetic
Reasons for Jew and Non-Jew
to Unite in Prayer*

CHAPTER ONE

A Unifying Prayer

The Standing Prayer, Shemonei Esrei, is the unifying form of worship for both the Jew and Gentile believers in Messiah Yeshua as well as Jews still looking for Messiah. This prayer is one spoken in faith by both those looking for Messiah's return and those looking for His arrival. It is a common prayer of all those who consider themselves children of Abraham, and the prayer of faith prayed by the Roman centurion Cornelius. The prayer meeting between Peter and Cornelius in Acts 10 had its beginning in Genesis 1, and that meeting is still unfolding in the lives of Jews and Christians today.

The standing prayer, the Amidah, is nicknamed the Shemoneh Esrei, which means "eighteen," and it is named for the original eighteen individual prayers that make up the service of the Shemoneh Esrei, which is prayed morning, afternoon, and evening. Daniel prayed three times daily facing Jerusalem, and Jews pray in the direction of the Holy City as well. Although the Jewish prayers were codified in the days of Gamaliel II and modified from time to time, Talmudic tradition attributes many of the oldest prayers of the Shemoneh Esrei to early Second Temple era. "The Shemoneh Esrei was instituted by the 120 men of the Great Assembly, among whom were the last of the Prophets."[1] The 120 men of the Great Assembly were gathered in the generation of Ezra and Nehemiah during the building of the Second Temple after the Babylonian captivity. It is this school of Biblical scholars who oversaw the spiritual direction of the Jewish people and who compiled many of the benedictions of the Shemoneh Esrei. As if to underline the spiritual significance of an emerging Third Temple constituted of the Body of Messiah Yeshua, the number of disciples gathered for prayer in the first chapter of Acts is 120 men and women. The Book of Acts contains numerous fulfillments of prophecy, especially chapters 10 and 11, the narrative of Cornelius and Peter's dynamic meeting.

The text of the Shemoneh Esrei varies a little at the three daily times of prayer, and it may be modified for Sabbath, high holy days, or for personal petitions for healing or fasting. If the last of the Older Testament prophets had influence on the framework of the Shemoneh Esrei, then the prayers have prophetic significance, perhaps according to the hours of prayer. The times of prayer correspond to the times of Temple sacrifice. The 3:00 P.M. prayers are offered at the time of the afternoon Temple sacrifices. Because they correspond to the offering time allotted for the *Minchah* offering, the allowed time of this prayer is from half-past the hour of noon until evening. Now that the sacrifices have ceased, the prayers are offered in lieu of the morning and evening sacrifices,[2] also known as the *tamid* offering. As the tamid sacrifice did not change from day to day in the Temple, neither does the repetition of the Shemoneh Esrei in the synagogue. "The core of every worship service in the synagogue is the Shemoneh Esrei. It is called Shemoneh Esrei because its daily form originally consisted of eighteen benedictions. This prayer constitutes

---

1. Rabbi Elie Munk, *The World of Prayer*, Trans. Henry Biberfield and Leonard Oschry (New York: P. Feldheim, 1954), 120.

2. Ibid, 22.

the essence of the daily morning, afternoon and evening services."[3] It is prayed standing and facing toward Jerusalem. The gospel of Mark 11:25 verifies this ancient posture of prayer: "*Whenever you stand praying, forgive, if you have anything against anyone, so that your Father who is in heaven will also forgive you your transgressions.*"

The Patriarch Isaac is credited with instituting the Minchah, or Three O'Clock Prayer, according to his evening (afternoon) meditation in the field.[4] Jacob instituted the evening prayers,[5] and Abraham the morning prayers.[6] The Minchah, or Isaac's prayer, unifies the Jew of the evening prayer, represented by Jacob, or Israel, with the Abrahamic Gentile nations of the morning prayer. "*And there was evening and there was morning, one day.*" In Abraham's binding of Isaac is a shadow of the Messiah, who comes to unify Israel and the nations who have faith in the Lamb and the Ram. He also brings into unity the prayers of the nations and the prayers of Israel. In one day, evening and morning are unified. This is why we find Jews, Peter and John, and the Gentile Cornelius at Minchah prayers in Acts. They are praying for the unification and restoration of all things in the Commonwealth of Israel.

"*And God called the light Day, and the darkness he called Night. There was setting, and there was dawning: one day.*"[7] The day is both light and darkness. Rabbi Isaac said, "At the Creation, God irradiated the world from end to end with the light, but then it was withdrawn, so as to deprive the sinners of the world of its enjoyment, and it is stored away for the righteous, as it stands written, 'Light is sown for the righteous;' then will the worlds be in harmony and all will be

---

3. Rabbi Hayim Halevy, *To Be a Jew*, (USA: Basic Books, 1972), 161.
4. Genesis 24:63.
5. Genesis 46:2.
6. Genesis 19:27.
7. Everett Fox, trans. *The Five Books of Moses*. (New York: Schocken, 1995), 13.

united into one, but until the future world is set up, this light is put away and hidden."[8] True Light is seen neither day nor night in this present world. After the Day of the Lord, however, the present darkness will cease, for Adonai himself will be the Light of New Jerusalem.[9] Until that Day, however, there is a distinction between night and day. Praying the Minchah prayer prophesies of the New Jerusalem, the Kingdom of Heaven, in which day and night cease, and the power of Adonai unifies all Israel in His Light. For this reason, the Minchah is offered when day and night merge.

Yeshua is the gate to the unified Kingdom. As the Passover Lamb, He was slain "between the evenings," or as sometimes translated, "afternoon."[10] In Second Temple times, the Passover lambs are offered by each family immediately following the evening tamid offering, which is slain an hour earlier, or approximately 1:30 P.M., and offered an hour later, 2:30 P.M. The Passover lambs are offered at about 3:00 P.M., the hour of prayer.[11] At the time when day and night merge, the Lamb, the unifying force of Day and Night, Jew and Gentile, is offered as a sacrifice. It is the sacrifice of the Lamb at Passover that opens the gate to unity. The evidence is the blood applied to the doorposts, the gate to the house, or rather, the House of Adonai.

---

8. Gershom Scholem, ed., *Zohar, the Book of Splendor*, (New York: Schocken, 1963), 5.

9. Revelation 21:23.

10. Rabbi Elie Munk, *The Call of the Torah*: Volume 2 Shemot. Trans. E.S. Mazer (Brooklyn, NY: Mesorah Publications, Ltd., 1994), 133.

11. Alfred Edersheim, *The Temple: Its Ministry and Services* (Peabody, MA: Hendrickson Publishers, 1994), 174.

CHAPTER TWO

Jew and Gentile:
Peter and Cornelius

The Shemoneh Esrei, whatever its form evolving in the Second Temple era, is a common prayer for both Jews and "God-fearers" in Acts of the Apostles. Peter and John observe the hour of prayer: "*Now Peter and John went up together into the temple at the hour of prayer, being the ninth hour.*"[12] In Acts, Peter and John are still accustomed to praying in the Temple at the appointed hour, and they encounter a lame man, likely a Jew, at the hour of Minchah prayer, the ninth hour. This is three o'clock. The lame man's inability to walk in the life of the covenant people makes him poor. He asks alms at the Beautiful Gate, and receives silver and gold of the Kingdom, which is strength to walk into the Temple of Israel as a strong man. His waiting for alms at the gate parallels the common term for a non-Jew who practices some of the *Torah*, but who has not yet converted to Judaism; he is a "proselyte of the gate." Although he is a native-born Israelite, there is yet a barrier between him and the inner Temple courts, for none blemished in body could enter into those precincts.

---

12. Acts 3:1, NAS.

The correlation to Minchah prayer and the poor lame man is found in Jewish law. In Berachot 34b of the Talmud, the code of Jewish law and commentary, we read, "The Minchah has the same high degree of holiness which is generally brought by a poor person." The reason is that a poor man may have to fast his daily bread in order to afford his offering, so his Minchah has a heightened degree of holiness. Adonai's concern for the poor is evidenced by the many provisions in Leviticus for the poor man to bring an offering of reduced cost, whether turtledoves and meal in place of flesh, or a single lamb instead of several. This poor man's Minchah request for help from the disciples of Yeshua is endowed with special favor from his Father in heaven.

Peter and John's Shemoneh Esrei prayers of faith at the three o'clock hour of Minchah minister healing to the poor lame man. This restored Jew sees the beautiful feet of Peter and John, who bring him the good news of Messiah Yeshua. He no longer has to sit outside the Beautiful Gate like a Gentile, but he can walk, leap, and praise Adonai in the Temple. Yeshua is the Beautiful Gate to the House of God. By faith in the blood of the Minchah Lamb, who was sacrificed at the hour of prayer as an everlasting memorial, the restored Israelite can enter the Temple on strong feet. The cripple is reunited with his Jewish brothers and his Messiah in the life of the covenant. He affirms the blessing of the Shemoneh Esrei, "Blessed are You, O Lord, who heals the sick your people Israel."[13]

Cornelius is also in Minchah prayer when he is visited by the angel. *"He saw in a vision evidently about the ninth hour of the day an angel of God coming in to him, and saying unto him, Cornelius."*[14] While many English readers would picture Cornelius as kneeling in prayer with clasped hands as Christians do today, the true picture would look much different. Cornelius learned of the One God of Israel from Israelites;

---

13. Munk, *World*, 137.
14. Acts 10:3.

therefore, he learned how to pray from Israelites! Picture Cornelius standing in his home facing Jerusalem. He takes three steps back, then three steps forward, symbolically stepping into the Presence of Adonai. He begins to pray, "My Adonai, open my lips, that my mouth may declare your praise..."

Cornelius' Minchah prayers are accompanied by acts of kindness to the Jews of his community. He offers not only the sacrifice of his lips, but good deeds of the *Torah*. The text calls Cornelius a "God-fearer." A God-fearer is a Gentile, a "proselyte of the gate," who has accepted the one God of Israel and who has begun to keep some of the commandments. Cornelius the God-fearer also observes the Jewish hour of prayer: "*And Cornelius said, 'Four days ago I was fasting until this hour; and at the ninth hour I prayed in my house, and, behold, a man stood before me in bright clothing.*"[15] In the waning decades of the Second Temple, the hour of prayer is the ninth hour. This places the prayer "between the evenings," between noon and sundown, three o'clock, the time of unity for day and night.

Even the time of month when Cornelius prayed is evident. Rabbi Munk reminds us, "The Torah ordains '*On your days of rejoicing and your holy days and on your month's beginning, you shall blow the trumpets over your offerings that they may be to you a memorial (zikaron) before your God.*"[16] Just as the Jews place goodwill money offerings in the Temple trumpets to accompany their prayers, Cornelius' good deeds are offered with prayer, and together they ascend as a memorial offering, a *zikaron*, for the angel says, "*Your prayers and gifts to the poor have come up as a **memorial offering** before God.*"[17] Cornelius' Minchah prayer and gifts to the poor parallel Peter's Minchah and gift to the poor, not silver and gold, but healing. *Rosh Chodesh*, the first day of the lunar Biblical

---

15. Acts 10:30, NAS.

16. Munk, *World*, 150.

17. Acts 10:4.

month, is a day appointed for sacrifices of prayer and good deeds to be an especial *zikaron* to Adonai. This may be Cornelius' exact day of prayer.

When one is fasting as Cornelius says he is the day of his visitation, a significant benediction of the Shemoneh Esrei is inserted. The fasting benediction is a fervent plea to Adonai to answer the prayer:

> Answer us, Adonai, answer us, on this day of our fast, for we are in great distress. Do not pay attention to our wickedness; do not hide Your Face from us, and do not ignore our plea. Please be near to our cry; please comfort us with your kindness—before we call to You answer us, as it is said: 'And it will be that *before they call, I will answer; while they are speaking, I will hear.*' For You, Adonai, are the One Who responds in time of distress, who redeems and rescues.[18]

The answer to Cornelius' fervent Minchah prayer is that indeed, while he is yet speaking, Adonai hears and answers. Cornelius is rewarded with not only acceptance of his *zikaron* offering of prayer, but redemption for his whole household, and the gate is opened for the unification of the Jew and Gentile in the Commonwealth of Israel. The Orthodox Jewish translation of the New Testament plainly connects the *zikaron* (remembrance) to the unification of Jew and Gentile through the sacrifice of Messiah. Paul urges the Ephesians:

> Have *zikaron* (remembrance) that you were at that time unrelated and separate from Rebbe, Melech HaMoshiach, having been alienated from the citizenship in the Am Berit, from Yisroel, being

---

18. Rabbi Nosson Scherman, Editor and Translator, *The Complete Artscroll Siddur*, (Brooklyn, NY: Mesorah Publications, Ltd., 1995), p. 265.

strangers to the Beritot HaHavtacha, <u>lost</u>, and having no tikvah (hope) and without G-d in the Olam Hazeh. But now in Rebbe, Melech HaMoshiach Yehoshua, you, who <u>formerly</u> were in the outermost courts, have been brought near by the kapparah of the dam of Moshiach... Therefore, then, <u>no longer</u> are you zarim and aliens, but **you are fellow-citizens** of the Kadoshim and **bnei bayit members of the household of G-d.**[19]

The KJV translates the same passage:

Therefore remember, that formerly you, the Gentiles in the flesh...that you were at that time separate from Christ, excluded from the commonwealth of Israel, and strangers to the covenants of promise, having no hope and without God in the world. But now in Christ Jesus you who formerly were far off have been brought near by the blood of Christ...For He Himself is our peace, who made both *groups into* **one**...that in Himself He might make the two into **one** new man...for through Him we both have our access in **one** Spirit to the Father. So then you are no longer strangers and aliens, but you are **fellow citizens with the saints, and are of God's household...**

Paul's placing of believing Gentiles within the *Am Berit,* or as most English translations read, the Commonwealth of Israel, and the Gentiles' inclusion with the *bnei bayit,* or Sons of the Household, gives credence to Rabbi Munk's comment on a portion of the Minchah Shemoneh Esrei: "The third group (of prayers) comprises the spiritual preconditions for the reunion of the nation of Israel under the rule of G-d.

19. *The Orthodox Jewish Brit Chadasha,* (New York: AFI International Publishers, 1996). 491.

According to the prediction of the prophets, the spiritual and moral foundation will have to be laid before the rehabilitation of our people can take place."[20] Cornelius' commandment-keeping, acts of kindness to the Jews, and participation in a "Jewish" prayer lay the moral foundation for the rescue and reunion of Israel under the rule of God.

---

20. Munk, *World*, 126.

CHAPTER THREE

Preparing for Messiah

ornelius' Minchah prayers hint of his preparation to move beyond the gate of the lame man. The Minchah, as a substitute for the *tamid* daily offering of blood sprinkled twice a day on the four corners of the altar, "expresses the readiness of the worshiper to surrender to the powers of His Body and Spirit, both as an individual and as a **member of the nation** to the Divine."[21] Cornelius' Minchah prayer expresses a desire for redemption from the Holy One of Israel and for grafting into the nation of Israel. The four corners of the altar or prayer represent the four corners of the earth.[22] This prayer acknowledges faith in the promise made to Abraham that all nations of the earth are blessed through Abraham's seed.

Cornelius is among the firstfruits of the Gentiles who will receive the blessing of Abraham, and the first to come home to the covenant through the Beautiful Gate of Yeshua. The sign of his readiness is the offering of good deeds to the Jews and his participation in a Jewish prayer, which is a personal

---

21. Ibid, 124.
22. Ibid, 123.

Temple service. Although formerly a proselyte of the gate, Cornelius moves beyond the Gentile court in faith. The Minchah prayer and good deeds of Torah are a sign of personal readiness for Messiah's coming.

According to Chofetz Chaim, one of the leading Jewish commentators on the arrival of Messiah, the prayers of the Shemoneh Esrei signal a personal preparedness for the coming of Messiah. He writes:

> What shame and embarrassment we will feel when Mashiach (Messiah) comes! We will have nowhere to hide our disgrace when it becomes apparent that we did not prepare ourselves. Then it will be known that all our prayers and petitions for his coming— those we utter three times a day in the Shemoneh Esrei and those we repeat whenever we recite the grace after meals—were not said with truth and sincerity. For had we really wanted Mashiach to come, wouldn't we have prepared ourselves?[23]

The prayers of the Shemoneh Esrei to the Jew represent the expectation of the Messiah. When a Jew sees a God-fearer praying the Shemoneh Esrei, he knows that Messiah's return is imminent.

Peter is on a rooftop "about noon" when he prays at the home of Shimon the Tanner. We know that Minchah may be offered as early as "half-hour past the half-day mark until sundown."[24] It may be that the stench from the tanning operations drives Peter to the rooftop to begin his prayers at the earliest time—for some of the tanning agents can include such ingredients as dog excrement! Peter falls into a trance,

---

23. Chofetz Chaim, *The Chofetz Chaim on Awaiting Messiah* (Southfield, MI: Targum Press, Inc., 1993), 62.

24. Abraham Cohen, *Everyman's Talmud*, (New York: Schocken Books, 1949), 163.

for how long the text is unclear, but we can guess he is experiencing his vision well into the time allotted for Minchah. The messengers from Cornelius arrive and "stood at the gate."[25] Like the poor man asking alms, the "proselytes of the gate" are on the threshold of breaking into the Household of God through the gospel of Yeshua.

Although the Gentiles come to the gate of a Jewish home seeking the gospel of Messiah, they do not become Jewish to hear the message. Peter goes with the Gentiles to Cornelius' home, and in violation of Jewish law (not the Torah!), crosses the threshold to proclaim the gospel. The Gentiles can also apply the unifying blood of the Lamb to their doorposts. They stand at the gate no longer, and they are unified with Israel, the House of God, for when the Passover lamb is eaten, "*those who gathered around it formed one family, just as the lamb itself was served whole.*"[26]

The Minchah prayers of the Shemoneh Esrei are a key to renewed expectation of Messiah. Cornelius, a Gentile, offers sacrifices of kindness to the Jewish community and fasting along with Minchah prayers. His prayer of unification results in the open gate of Messiah to the Gentiles. It serves as a *zikaron*, reminding El Shaddai of His promise to Abraham. If once again the faithful Gentiles do deeds of kindness for the Jewish community, keep Yeshua's commandments, fast, and offer Minchah prayers that affirm faith in the arrival of Messiah and His restoration of Israel, then it may be that we open the gate for Messiah's return, and the unity of our faith will be established.

Jews around the world pray the Shemoneh Esrei daily. Somewhere in the world, right now, Jews are praying for the coming of Messiah. "*From the rising of the sun until the going down of the same, the Name of the Lord is to be praised.*"[27] This

---

25. Acts 10:17.

26. Edersheim, 183.

27. Psalm 113:3, KJV.

prayer for the Kingdom to come begins with "*Shema (Hear!), O Israel. The Lord your God; the Lord is One.*" If Jewish and Gentile believers lack the power of Peter and Cornelius to have prayers answered, then they must look to the most powerful move of the Holy Spirit. The power was present when Jew and Gentile believers in Messiah offered daily corporate prayer for the restoration of Israel, and they were zealous for the commandments of the Torah. The four corners of the earth will shake with the expectation and healing power of Yeshua manifest when Jews and Gentiles unite in prayer.

CHAPTER FOUR

Eighteen

Eighteen Benedictions were chosen for the Shemonei Esrei because in the Hebrew Scriptures, numbers are not incidental. They may function as symbols, have gematria value that alludes to other words of the same value, or have prophetic implications. Although some occult practices use "lucky numbers" and such, Biblical gematria is not fortune-telling, but significance-telling. In Scripture, painstaking care is given to the number of years a king reigned or an ancestor lived, the number of days surrounding significant events, or day and years concerning prophetic decrees. Studying the significance of Scriptural numbers should not be confused with learning mystical arts. Instead, allow the Scripture to define the significance of the number eighteen. The number eighteen alludes to the binding and loosing of the strong men of Israel.

Yeshua spoke to His disciples: "*Whatsoever you bind on earth...whatsoever you loose...in my Name...*"[28] In its Hebraic context, the terms "binding and loosing" refer to the making of *halakha*, or Jewish law. If the rabbis "loose," they permit an

---

28. Matthew 18:18-20.

action to be done. If they "bind," they do not permit it to be done. In Yoma 39a, ancient Jewish law states, "Judicial power must be exercised with due recognition of the principle that the Torah is considerate of property rights." The safeguarding of private property applied especially to laws of *issur* and *heter*, 'bind and loosing,' i.e. to ritual and ceremonial matters."[29] According to the genuine meaning of binding and loosing, Yeshua gives authority to two or three believing disciples to judge practical matters of walking out the Torah.

In Luke 13:11-16, a "daughter of Abraham" has been bound for eighteen years. Her infirmity has prevented her from being able to walk in the fullness of Torah, which is covenant life. Her inability to walk in the Word has manifested itself in her body. "*A broken spirit is as rottenness of the bones.*"[30] The spiritual Torah, the life-giving Word, restores broken spirits, bones, and blood. If the children of Abraham are loosed to walk in the spirit of the Torah written on their hearts according to the terms of the New Covenant in Jeremiah 31, then like the infirm daughter of Abraham, physical strength is restored. This woman was infirm for eighteen years.

Other passages where Yeshua discusses binding and loosing is the binding of the strong man:

> Or else how can one enter into a strong man's
> house, and spoil his goods, except he first bind the
> strong man? and then he will spoil his house. [31]

> No man can enter into a strong man's house, and
> spoil his goods, except he will first bind the strong
> man; and then he will spoil his house.[32]

---

29. George Horowitz, *The Spirit of Jewish Law, A Brief Account of Biblical and Rabbinical Jurisprudence*, (New York: Bloch Publishing, 1993), 103.

30. Proverbs 17:22.

31. Matthew. 12:29.

32. Mark 3:27.

A strong man has a house. In order to take possession of the house, the enemy first binds the strong man. Demons and the devil don't have houses. Human beings have a physical vessel containing the soul and spirit that comprises their house, or as Paul calls them, temples of the Holy Spirit and jars of clay. The enemy wants to take a strong man's house because as long as he controls even the door to the house, a human cannot operate effectively in the life-giving spirit of the Word. For this reason, Yeshua says after one repents and sweeps the house clean, or purifies himself from the Kingdom of Death, he must immediately start to furnish the house with things of the Holy Spirit. He must start moving in the furniture of the Word of God.

A vacuum constantly seeks to be filled. The human house is a spiritual vacuum, and it will either absorb the Holy Spirit, or an unholy spirit. It will not exist perpetually in a vacuum. Yeshua warns the hearer to discourage the return of the unclean spirit by not merely sweeping the house clean, but by furnishing it just as the physical Temple. The individual's house-Temple requires an altar of sacrifice for crucifying the flesh, a laver for the washing and purifying water of the Word, an incense altar of prayer, a table to break bread with fellow Israelites, a menorah filled with oil for the illumination of the Ruach HaKodesh, and the most holy article of all, the voice of the Almighty speaking intimate Living Words from between the two cherubim, breathing life to His commandments in the heart of the believer.

If the enemy wants to take over the house, he must bind the strong man from entering the Temple courts with praise and from keeping the commandments of the Torah. If the strong man is loosed, he is permitted to praise and to keep the Torah written on his heart. The opening prayer of the Shemoneh Esrei says, "My Lord, open my lips that my mouth may declare your praise." How long has it been since a Gentile learned this prayer? In the history of the church, the deceiver bound the strong man of the house early. He convinced the

Church Fathers to bind Yeshua's assemblies from keeping the fullness of the Torah so that they could dissociate from "Jewish customs," such as the Biblical festivals and Sabbath, which are not customs at all, but God's eternal Word. For this reason, believers in Yeshua remained in a state of infirmity for a little less than eighteen hundred years, dating from the time Gentiles began to dominate the congregations. The Gentile domination occurs around the time the disciples of the original twelve disciples died, such as Polycarp, John's disciple. By the second century, these "great lights" are extinguished, and no longer are those with first-hand knowledge of "Christian" observance available to influence the formation of practice and doctrine, which we might also call Christian *halakha*.[33]

The Church Fathers promoted a doctrine alleging that Adonai's law, His Torah, His teaching and instruction to a holy people, was somehow bondage and unbelief. It became something less than the *"perfect law of liberty"* described by the Lord's brother James in his epistle to the twelve tribes scattered abroad. In this generation, however, those who were bound from the Torah are being loosed. Where the Spirit of the Lord is, there is liberty to keep His commandments! This liberty is originating in the Hebraic Roots and Messianic movements under the inspiration of the Holy Spirit, the *Ruach HaKodesh*.

Some passages from the Torah and Judges of Israel give us additional interpretive keys to the strong man. The role of the golden calf in Israel's history is a metaphor of mixed worship, for the Israelites worshiped the calf as the "god" who brought them up out of Egypt. The calf is unacceptable because Adonai does not accept any other god beside Him, although the Israelites claimed to worship Him through it. Adonai will not share His glory with a calf, neither with Oestre, although she is not the god Gentiles worship at Easter.

---

33. Dan Gruber, *The Church and the Jews*, (Serenity Books, 1997), 22.

The example of Sinai and even the Apostle Paul's words are clear about remaining free from the influence of idols. In 2 Corinthians 6:16, Paul reminds us, *"Or what agreement has the temple of God with idols? For we are the temple of the living God; just as God said, "'I will dwell in them and walk among them; And I will be their God, and they shall be My people.'"* The writer of 1 John 5:21 pleads with us in the final words before the apocalyptic words of Revelation, *"Little children, keep yourselves from idols. Amen."* In Revelation 2:14, the church is warned once more, *"But I have a few things against you, because you have there some who hold the teaching of Balaam, who kept teaching Balak to put a stumbling block before the sons of Israel, to eat things sacrificed to idols, and to commit acts of immorality."*

How does the church today eat things sacrificed to idols? Have you ever eaten an Easter egg? How did the church allow a pagan goddess' name to replace the names of Adonai's appointed days to celebrate Yeshua's sacrifice and victory as the Passover Lamb and the Firstfruits from the dead? Most Christians will say that they do not worship Easter, but they worship God! Isn't that what the Israelites said? Do the writers of the New Testament accept this excuse? Will Yeshua? Yeshua said a day would come when his people would worship in spirit and in truth. Can we say that we have the "spirit" of Easter yet neglect the truth that its observance blends pagan and Biblical ritual?

No one could doubt a true believer's salvation which is received by faith in Yeshua alone, but there are serious doubts as to the Christian's ability to walk as a strong man in Israel. Many believers today walk in bondage to the sickly, lame customs and expectations of the modern world, a bondage from which Yeshua has already released them if they would only walk in freedom. Israel was a saved and redeemed people from the slavery of Egypt, yet their mixed worship weakened their nation and subjected them to the servitude from which their Father had already delivered them. Will no one stand up in this late hour to urge on the Church to worship in spirit and truth? Yeshua is willing to break the bonds of his captive people once again.

Be of good courage, little children. Some leaders in mainstream Christianity are standing up. A news article from the April 26, 2002, edition of the *Jerusalem Post* must have caused no small stir among Jews and Gentiles alike:

> "We are sweeping the paganism of Easter out of the Church and applying the seasons of God," said CBN TV WorldReach host Christine Darg, who led over 200 Christians from 15 nations in a Passover conference at the King David Hotel in Jerusalem. Easter actually predates Christianity, so we are no longer saying 'Happy Easter,' because the Word of God says, 'Do not even allow the names of foreign deities to be upon our lips.'"

Like the Israelites struggling with the golden calf at Sinai, Gentiles will only regain their first century strength and anointing in pure, not mixed worship. The prophetic message of Judges 3 speaks to this generation:

> And the children of Israel did evil again in the sight of the LORD: and the LORD strengthened Eglon the king of Moab against Israel, because they had done evil in the sight of the LORD. And he gathered unto him the children of Ammon and Amalek, and went and smote Israel. So the children of Israel served Eglon the king of Moab eighteen years…Eglon smote Israel and possessed the city of palm trees.[34]

The Israelite judge Ehud's overthrow of King Eglon involves a ploy to speak to King Eglon alone, and then Judge

---

34. Judges 3:12-25.

Ehud stabs King Eglon with his dagger. King Eglon is so obese that the fat closes over the dagger, and Ehud escapes before Eglon's subjects know that he is dead, not using the toilet as they suppose from the stench of the waste from his bowels. In Hebrew, *Eglon* is "calf-like." *Ehud* is "undivided union." The judge Ehud is the son of *Gera*, which is "grain." Palm trees in Scripture represent the righteous.[35] The king "Like a Calf" possesses the righteous for eighteen years. Then an Undivided Union, Son of Grain, overthrows one Like a Calf. The Word of God is a sharp, two-edged dagger by which mixed worship is defeated. The King Like a Calf is so fat, that the fat occludes Ehud's dagger. The overweight, prosperity-addicted members of the church will be dead for some time before anyone subject to the calf-like worship notices, for mixed worship conceals the true Word of God. The text states the "dirt" came out. The sword of the Spirit, the Word of God, will expose the uncleanness of our clay vessels. It will allow the unclean things that have not been purged to spill out.

To overthrow the influence of the worship system like a calf, Jews and Gentiles, the Sons of Grain, the sons of the Word of God, must acknowledge the unity of God, the Undivided Union, through the greatest commandment, the *Shema*, "*Hear O Israel; the Lord your God; the Lord is One.*" We then progress through unified prayer for redemption from the One who said, "*I and the Father are One.*" It is a mixture of paganism and truth that blasphemes the Name and Undivided Union. Cornelius' and Peter's prayer, the Shemoneh Esrei, affirms faith in the Undivided Union to overthrow the enemy. After eighteen years, the Lord raises up a Judge in Israel. One benediction of the Shemonei Esrei pleads, "Restore our judges as in earliest times, and our counselors as at first." Pray for judges in Israel to rise up and break the eighteen hundred years of oppression and binding of the Torah!

---

35. Psalm 92:12.

33

Another proof that eighteen units is a Scriptural limit to Israel's oppression is Judges 10:6-16, of which the most notable verse is, *"And that year they vexed and oppressed the children of Israel: eighteen years, all the children of Israel that were on the other side Jordan in the land of the Amorites, which is in Gilead."* This strong deliverer arrives after eighteen years, or eighteen units of mixed worship in Israel. He restores strength to Israel to walk in the Torah. *"So they put away the foreign gods from among them and served the LORD; and He could bear the misery of Israel no longer."*[36] Are Christians today vexed by their enemies? Let them put away the foreign gods from among them, and your Father in Heaven will bear your misery no longer.

---

36. Judges 10:16.

CHAPTER FIVE

Eighteen and the Strong Man

Yet another passage teaching the significance of the number eighteen is "*And Meshelemiah [whom God repays] had sons and brethren, strong men, eighteen.*"[37] The number of a strong group of sons and brethren is eighteen. The name Meshelemiach, "God Repays," has significance. The name Jerusalem, or *Yerushalayim* has a double implication in Hebrew. Not only is it a place of *shalom*, peace, but the root word *shalem*, "he repays," implies that God will repay or fulfill completely in that place. When El Shaddai passes the burning torch between the carcasses in the covenant he cuts with Abraham, He puts Abraham to sleep, which means that if Abraham or his descendants break the covenant, then God Himself must repay. Of course the covenant was broken, and in the place Yerushalayim, El Shaddai repaid and fulfilled the broken covenant with the blood of His own Son, who did not come to abolish, but to *fulfill* the covenant of the Torah. It is through the blood of the same Son that our bondage is broken and we are loosed to keep His commandments. He repaid His good to us for

---

37. 1 Chronicles 26:9.

our evil in Yerushalayim. The One Who Repays is looking for eighteen strong men.

Ezra's rebuilding of the Temple after the Babylonian captivity is another allusion to the significance of eighteen.

> And I sent them with commandment unto Iddo the chief at the place Casiphia, and I told them what they should say unto Iddo, and to his brethren the Nethinims, at the place **Casiphia** (silvery; of silver), that they should bring unto us ministers for the house of our God. And by the good hand of our God upon us they brought us a man of understanding, of the sons of Mahli, the son of Levi, the son of Israel; and Sherebiah (God has scorched), with his sons and his brethren, eighteen.[38]

Eighteen is a strong community of ministers to a congregation who desire to rebuild a fallen Temple. The number eighteen is a link to the passage in Chronicles. Adonai intended to repay in Yerushalayim with the blood of His Son, and indeed He did. That blood was bought in an earthly sense for silver, *kesef*, from Judas, and that *kesef* later buys a Potter's Field of Blood for strangers, or non-Jews.[39] An important image is that of Yeshua overthrowing the tables of the moneychangers, those who traded in *kesef*, silver, in the Temple, which was the place where the strong men should minister in the House of our God that will one day become a "house of prayer for all nations."[40] Like Machli, these are men of understanding, like the Levites, men of purity, and like Sherebiach, men scorched in the refining fires, a total of eighteen strong men, ready to lead all Israel in pure worship. They leave Casiphia, the money-changers' tables, and facilitate the worship of both rich and poor in the Temple courts.

---

38. Ezra 8:17
39. Matthew 27:7
40. Mark 11:17.

The bound woman affirms that Israel's limit to infirmity is eighteen:

> And, behold, there was a woman which had a spirit of infirmity eighteen years, and was bowed together, and could in no wise lift up herself. And ought not this woman, being a daughter of Abraham, whom Satan has bound, lo, these eighteen years, be loosed from this bond on the Sabbath day?[41]

Yeshua looses the daughters of Abraham in the nineteenth year. Christian believers may have been bound from keeping the fullness of the Torah, but when all believers pray the Shemoneh Esrei, "grant us our portion in your Torah..." the Commonwealth of Israel furnishes the Temple with the good things from God's Word. The enemy has spoiled the houses and stolen peace, health, and strength. It is time for all sons and daughters of Abraham to grow strong in the Living Word. The number of freedom and strength is eighteen.

The strong are those who "*observe to do according to all the Torah, which Moses my servant commanded thee.*"[42] It is the portion of strong Israel with their Messiah, "*Therefore will I divide him a portion with the great, and he shall divide the spoil with the strong; because he has poured out his soul unto death: and he was numbered with the transgressors; and he bore the sin of many, and made intercession for the transgressors.*"[43] Faith in the work of this Messiah makes the sick strong. "*And through faith in his name hath made this man strong, whom ye see and know: yea, the faith which is by him hath given him this perfect soundness in the presence of you all.*"[44]

---

41. Luke 13:11-16.
42. Joshua 1:7.
43. Isaiah 53.
44. Acts 3:16.

CHAPTER SIX

Open My Lips

Jewish custom is to pray the Shemoneh Esrei as a silent, or barely audible prayer based on I Samuel 1:13-15. Channah prays, and the High Priest Eli sees only her lips moving, so he concludes that she is drunk. She is, however, pouring out her heart to Adonai. The Shemonei Esrei is preceded by a request, "*My Lord, open my lips, that my mouth may declare Your Praise.*" It is a request based on Psalm 34:14, and it begs for the ability to pour out the concerns of the heart as Channah. The Hebrew word for "praise" in the request is "*tehilla.*" Scriptural praise is throughout the Shmonei Esrei. If one prays in Hebrew, he prays Hebrew words that include many specific praises, including the *todah, hallal,* and *tehillah,* and he bows and bends the knee in *barak* praise.

Tehillah praise is to sing and laud in a form of high praise. It is on this form of praise that Yah is enthroned.[45] To this type of praise Paul refers when he warns believers not to be drunk, but to be filled with the Spirit and speak in Psalms, hymns, and spiritual songs.[46] The linguistic connection to

---

45. Psalm 22:3.
46. Ephesians 5:18-19.

Channah's prayer is the appearance of drunkenness. It is *tehillah* praise requested in the Shemonei Esrei. The disciples in Acts 2 probably entered this form of praise in their prayer in the Temple. Note that when the phenomenon of Acts 2 occurs, the Jewish believers are not in an upper room as in chapter 1. When the text says that they were gathered in "the house," this is a Hebraic reference to The House, a metaphor for The Temple. Some translations read, "the place," which is another Hebrew reference to the Temple Mount, known as *HaMakom*. The believers of Acts often gathered in Solomon's Porch to pray and preach, and we know that the Temple is The House where they gathered because of the huge numbers who were baptized. Only the Temple complex of numerous *mikvaot* could accommodate three thousand baptisms in one day. Interestingly, the Hebrew *mikveh*, which in English is translated baptism, has a double meaning. It is also a Hebrew word for hope. The three thousand who were baptized on Pentecost were immersed into the Mikveh Yisrael, the Hope of Israel, Messiah Yeshua. When the *Ruach HaKodesh* falls on the disciples during morning prayers, they speak in other tongues, and are accused of being drunk.

There is a connection between the gift of tongues and the Shemonei Esrei, which the disciples had gathered to pray that morning at morning prayers in the Temple. The Holy Spirit opened their lips, and they were declaring the *tehillah* praises of God in Jerusalem, just as they had requested the ability to do in the opening line of the Shemoneh Esrei. This group of people experienced the dynamic power of the Holy One of Israel. What did they have in common?

- They walked with Yeshua, and had a revelation of Him as the Messiah of Israel.
- They are Jews from Judah; Judah means "praiser" from *yadah, Yehudah.*
- They keep Torah, not necessarily according to Pharisaic tradition, but Scriptural Judaism. Many were *am*

haeretz, but even this common man's keeping of Torah was strict, for Peter states he's never eaten anything common or unclean.[47]

- They are keeping the Scriptural festivals, most particularly Shavuot, or Pentecost.
- They are commanded and commissioned by Yeshua Himself to go and make disciples of all nations, to teach them everything He had commanded them.
- They share a belief that Yeshua's blood ratified the New Covenant, and that the Torah is now written on their hearts according to Jeremiah 31:33.

Based on this common identity, the disciples need one additional thing in order to carry out the Great Commission. They need the ability to proclaim Yeshua as the Living Torah, the Word of God made flesh, and to praise the works of the Almighty. The gift of tongues enables them to do it. The gift of tongues is a sign that the Holy Spirit is in them. Holy, or *Kadosh,* means to be a sanctuary God can dwell in. If the gift of tongues is a sign of the Holy Spirit, then it is something that prepares the house of this body to be a sanctuary in which God can dwell. The Spirit of *kiddushin,* Holiness, the *Ruach HaKodesh,* places the furniture of the Temple in the sanctuary so that the person and God can dwell together in their House.

Around 1900, the gift of tongues manifested itself again in places such as Wales and Azusa Street.[48] The number of those who have opened their lips to declare the Lord's praise has grown steadily since. One of the characteristics of these "spirit filled" believers is that they have an intense hunger for the Word of God, at least initially.[49] If Messiah's return is

---

47. Acts 11:8.

48. James Bartleman, *What Really Happened at Azusa Street?,* (Northridge, CA: Voice Christian Publications, Inc., 1962), 6.

49. Bartleman, 30.

drawing near to this generation, then the bonds should be falling from the strong men so that they are loosed to keep the Torah. The prophet Zechariah says,

> Thus saith the LORD of hosts; In those days it shall come to pass, that ten men shall take hold out of all languages of the nations, even shall take hold of the skirt of him that is a Jew, saying, "We will go with you: for we have heard that God is with you."[50]

Not only have ten men, but tens of thousands of Gentiles are taking hold of the prayer shawl of Yeshua and acknowledging that God is with the Jews, and that the Jews have guarded the commandments of the Torah for the ingathering of Israel. Christian televangelists and preachers are appearing to their audiences and congregants wearing and teaching about the Jewish prayer shawl. While in Acts it was tens of thousands of Jews and those with the Jews who believed and who were all zealous for the Torah, today it is a joint movement of tens of thousands of Jews and Gentiles who have believed, and they are all zealous for the Torah.[51] As one, they take hold of the garment of The Jew, our Messiah Yeshua.

The gift of tongues is a harbinger of the modern "Messianic" movement. In Zechariah, specifically it is the *tallit*, or prayer garment, that Gentiles are grabbing; it is the Jewish prayer garment that puts the Jew and Gentile on the same path of hope. This is why it is so important to fervently pray and unite in "Jewish" prayer like Cornelius.

Messiah Yeshua promises us that the Holy Spirit teaches us all things. *"But the Helper, the Holy Spirit, whom the Father will send in My name, He will teach you all things, and bring to your remembrance all that I said to you."*[52] "Things" in Hebrew

---

50. Zechariah 8:23.
51. Acts 21:20.
52. John 14:26.

is *devarim*. Devarim is also the Hebrew name of the Book of Deuteronomy! In Hebrew, it also means "words" as well as "things." Yeshua is hinting at things with the words. He says the gift of the Holy Spirit is to learn "all things": He's hinting that the Holy Spirit will teach us all of the Book of Deuteronomy, the summary of all Torah in the form of an ancient covenant.[53] That is the Light we are to carry to the Nations: The *Davar HaElohim*, the Word that He commanded us! The Prophet Jeremiah promises this: "*But this is the covenant that I will make with the house of Israel after those days, says the Lord: I will put My law (Torah) in their minds, and write it on their hearts; and I will be their God, and they shall be My people.*"

This confirms what the prophet Ezekiel says is the sign of the Holy Spirit of the New Covenant: "*I will put My Spirit within you and cause you to walk in My statutes (mishpatim), and you will be careful to observe My ordinances (chukim).*"[54] What does the Holy Spirit cause a believer to do? To keep the commandments of Adonai! *Chukim and mishpatim* are the finer points of the Torah, including both moral commandments and commandments we don't understand. Are you a New Covenant believer? Are you being drawn by the Holy Spirit to keep the commandments of God?

---

53. Ariel and D'vorah Berkowitz, *Torah Rediscovered*, (Littleton, Colorado: First Fruits of Zion, Inc., 1996), 8.
54. Ezekiel 36:27

PART II

*The Prayers of the Shemoneh
Esrei with an Explanation of
Their Messianic Messages and
the Names of God*

CHAPTER SEVEN

Avot
The Fathers

Blessed are You, Adonai our God, and the God of our fathers, God of Abraham, God of Isaac, and God of Jacob. The Great, Mighty, and Awe-inspiring God, the Most High God, Who bestows kindness and creates all, Who remembers the kindnesses of the fathers, and Who brings a Redeemer to their children's children for the sake of His Name with love. O King, Helper, Savior, and Shield. Blessed are You, Adonai, Shield of Abraham.

The first benediction acknowledges not the Church Fathers or Fathers of the World (Jewish Talmudic sages) as our fathers, but Father Abraham.

> Listen to me, you who pursue righteousness, who seek the LORD: Look to the rock from which you were hewn and to the quarry from which you were dug. Look to Abraham your father and to Sarah who gave birth to you in pain; When {he} {was but} one I called him, Then I blessed him and multiplied him... pay attention to Me, O My people, and give ear to Me, O My nation; For a law will go forth from Me, And I will set My justice for a light of the peoples.

My righteousness is near, My salvation has gone
forth, And My arms will judge the peoples; the coast-
lands will wait for Me.[55]

Abraham is the rich heritage of both Jews and "the peoples." Jews and Gentiles acknowledge Abraham as the first person to clearly recognize God on his own. Ezekiel says of him,
"*Echad hayah Avraham,*" "Abraham was one [alone]." A non-
Jew prays this prayer because Adonai promises Abraham, "*I
have made you the father of a multitude of nations.*"[56] The
Mishnah and Tosefta, recorded opinions of the Jewish sages,
agree that even a convert is considered a descendant of
Abraham and may call the God of Israel the God of my
fathers.[57] Rabbi Shaul agrees with them in Galatians 3:7
"*Therefore, be sure that it is those who are of faith who are sons
of Abraham.*" Not only the faithful, but even the hopelessly lost
call Abraham Father: "*And he cried out and said, 'Father
Abraham, have mercy on me, and send Lazarus so that he may
dip the tip of his finger in water and cool off my tongue, for I am
in agony in this flame.'*"[58] It is not ethnicity that qualifies one
to call Abraham father, but doing the works of Abraham.
"*They answered and said to Him, Abraham is our father.*" Jesus
said to them, "*If you are Abraham's children, do the deeds of
Abraham.*"[59] In Romans 4:1-18, Paul gives the complete foundation for praying the Avot, whether Jew or non-Jew.

Is this blessing then on the circumcised, or on the
uncircumcised also? For we say, "faith was credited to
Abraham as righteousness." How then was it credited? While he was circumcised or uncircumcised?

---

55. Isaiah 51:1-5.
56. Genesis 17:5.
57. Berurah 49, 50.
58. Luke 16:24.
59. John 8:39.

Not while circumcised, but while uncircumcised; and he received the sign of circumcision, a seal of the righteousness of the faith which he had while uncircumcised, so that he might be the father of all who believe without being circumcised, that righteousness might be credited to them, and the father of circumcision to those who not only are of the circumcision, **but who also follow in the steps of the faith of our father Abraham which he had while uncircumcised.**[60]

Another important reason to pray in the remembrance of Abraham, Isaac, and Jacob is to define to which God we pray. The ecumenical movement proposes that all religions pray to the same god. Since in English there is a name so loosely used and profaned as "god," we specifically define the God to whom we pray as the God of Abraham, Isaac, and Jacob. "*I shall remember my covenant with Jacob, as well as my covenant with Isaac, as well as my covenant with Abraham will I remember.*"[61] The Hebrew word for "remember," *zikaron*, is a direct link from the patriarchs to Cornelius' Mincha prayer becoming a *zikaron*, a remembrance. Using the names of the three patriarchs reminds all the faithful to remember the covenant, and that if one does not relate to Adonai in covenant relationship, then he does not relate to the God of Abraham, Isaac, and Jacob.

An additional reason for petitioning the God of Abraham, Isaac, and Jacob is the way in which Adonai introduces Himself and His Name to Moses in Exodus 3. When He is reintroduced to the children of Israel, He is very specific about His identity: the El (God) of Abraham, Isaac, and Jacob. In Exodus 3:1-16, three times the Holy One identifies Himself as the God of Abraham, Isaac, and Jacob.

---

60. Romans 4:9-12.
61. Leviticus 26:42.

To the Jew, the three patriarchs represent attributes of kindness, strength or fear of heaven, and truth and balance. By invoking their names in remembrance, Israel asks to be imbued with these attributes. These principles are taught throughout the New Testament as well. If the root of all evil and sin is covetousness, then the root of all good and good deeds must be selflessness. The very definition of grace, or *chesed*, is selflessness, to live for a cause outside and greater than one's self. A *Chassid* is a selfless one. The Chassid studies the ways of God constantly in order to find ways to please his father. There are "God Chasers," but the children of Abraham, Isaac, and Jacob are God Pleasers. They give to others because they know it pleases God.

Each benediction of the Shemoneh Esrei contains powerful Names of God that define His attributes. These Names defend us[62] in a day of trouble, enable us to properly praise Him,[63] and put our enemies under our feet.[64] In our daily lives as well as our prayer time, one either sanctifies God's Name by his conduct or profanes it. To profane the Name is to be disobedient to His Word, not just in the Land of Israel, but especially to continue disobedience to Him in the lands of dispersion.[65] The impact of the Name is promised to Yeshua's disciples: *"But the* Helper, *the Holy Spirit, whom the Father will send in My name, He will teach you all* things, *and bring to your remembrance all that I said to you.*[66] A "helper" in Hebrew is *ozer*, and in John 14:26, the *Ozer* is defined as the *Ruach HaKodesh*, or Holy Spirit, one of the Names of God. *Ozer* is one of the Names of God in the Avot benediction.

Other Names of God in the benediction are *Melekh* (King), *Moshiah* (Savior), and *Magen Avraham* (Shield of Abraham).

---

62. Psalm 20.
63. Psalm 48:10.
64. Psalm 44:1-8.
65. Ezekiel 36:18-38.
66. John 14:26.

In Hebraic thought, the Name *Moshiah* is for the absolutely helpless. He saves us when we do not have the ability to move one finger to save ourselves. All who come to the Savior are children of Abraham in this respect; we enter the covenant completely helpless and motivated by faith alone. On the other hand, there are believers who have taken on the yoke of the Kingdom and who voluntarily endanger themselves to hold ground and advance the Kingdom of Heaven. They are volunteers in Adonai's service. In such instances, God becomes *Magen*, or shield. The function of the Magen Name is to request supernatural help in accomplishing missions for the Kingdom and protection for the mission. Faith is a shield. Without the faith of Father Abraham, it is impossible to please God. When Avram vanquishes the four kings in Canaan, Adonai assures him, *"Fear not, Avram, I am your shield; your reward is very great."*[67] Personal risk makes a believer partners with Adonai, and he may need the help of Magen Avraham.

Another Name of God in this benediction is *Goel*, or Redeemer: "And who brings a *Goel* to their children's children for His name's sake with love." This phrase is written in the present tense, and alludes to the Messiah as the Kinsman Redeemer. The Kinsman Redeemer was a close family member who took responsibility for his family's welfare. The Goel would take vengeace on the manslayer who killed someone under the Goel's care, and he would also take responsibility for redeeming a family member sold into servitude. Not only was Yeshua sent as a Redeemer to his family on earth at a specific time in history, He continues to redeem us because of His eternal nature. As long as Yeshua lives, His redemption as our *Goel* continues. Our Redeemer is redeeming us from bondage, and holds us safely in His hand until the complete redemption of our bodies and his vengeance is loosed on the enemies of his family.

---

67. Genesis 15:1.

The Avot benediction ends as most Hebrew blessings, "*Baruch atah Adonai* …" or "Blessed Are You O Lord…" Specifically it closes, "*Baruch atah Adonai, Magen Avraham.*" The sum of all the Hebrew words of the closing blessings is 113. This corresponds to the song of Channah in I Samuel 2:1-10, and the 113 times the word *lev*, or heart, is mentioned in the Torah. Again a connection to Channah's "drunken" prayer and the Shemoneh Esrei exists.

CHAPTER EIGHT

Gevurot
The Resurrection
Power of God

You are forever mighty, my Lord, the Reviver of the Dead are You, great in salvation. He makes the wind blow and He makes the rain fall. He upholds the living in kindness, resurrects the dead with great mercy, supports the fallen, heals the sick, and is faithful with those who sleep in the dust. Who is like you, Master of Powerful Deeds, and who can compare to You, King, who causes death, and restores life, and makes Salvation sprout! And you are faithful to resurrect the dead. Blessed are You, Adonai, Resurrection of the Dead.

The second blessing represents the memory of Isaac, and a glimpse of the final resurrection, which is pictured by Isaac at Mt. Moriah. While some think of Abraham as stopping the sacrifice before Isaac is harmed, the Jewish way of looking at it is that figuratively, Isaac was raised from the dead, for Abraham believed that El Shaddai would do so even if Abraham took Isaac's life.[68]

The resurrection from the dead is a major tenet of faith in Messiah Yeshua.[69] There is an interesting passage in the

---

68. Hebrews 11:17-19.
69. John 11:25.

Peshitta, which is the Aramaic translation of the New Testament even older than most surviving fragments of the Greek text. In the Murdock translation of the Peshitta, Matthew 1:21 states, "*...and she will bear a son; and thou shalt call his name Jesus (Yeshua), for he will **resuscitate** his people from their sins.*" The usual English translations from the Greek read, "*...He will **save** His people from their sins.*" While Yeshua's saving power is important, and indeed, the Name Yeshua literally means Salvation, the Aramaic text hints to us that the salvation specifically is a power of resuscitation from the death of sin. Messiah's CPR technique is unrivaled in bringing the dead to life!

This blessing reminds the supplicant daily that he lives in two realms, this one and the hereafter. While many live their lives with only casual attention to the other realm, a believer spends his or her life with ever-present consciousness of the realms of life and death, for he is commanded to choose life every day in faithfulness to the one who will one day resuscitate him from physical death. To aid a believer in his walk, he is given the Torah, and specifically the book of Leviticus, to teach the difference between clean and unclean, which raises awareness of the realm of death and prepares for resurrection to life. It is through studying, and as much as possible observing, these Levitical rituals that one acquires a consciousness of resurrection each day. Each day, this benediction reminds the faithful to choose life that he might live.

Anyone who prays this prayer of resurrection power with sincerity should feel renewed, because prayer restores vitality to both body and soul. It is the opportunity for daily resurrection in both physical and spiritual worlds. While humans use and abuse power in order to kill, maim, torture and imprison, or weaken their rivals, *El Gibor* uses His power to support the fallen, heal the sick, and release the confined. He even maintains His faith to those asleep in the dust, or those who can no longer be resuscitated from sickness by the intervention of man.[70] Messiah's complete work will be to rebuild all that is fallen in Israel, just as this prayer affirms daily.

In addition to resurrection power, the prayer acknowledges other revitalizing powers of *El Gibor*, one of the Names of God in this prayer. Another resurrecting power is His rain and His wind. The rain is God's blessing of prosperity and "truth from heaven, not by means of force or man's knowledge." Dew is that Word of Truth made clear and easily understood.[71] The wind, or Holy Spirit, *Ruach HaKodesh*, scatters the seeds of the Word of God across the earth. Rain causes the buried seed to rot and disintegrate, but afterward it germinates into a beautiful plant, just as our resurrected bodies are planted in the earth but will emerge in a much superior form. As Scripture says, *"it remains to be revealed what we shall be."*[72] This physical body is just a seed form of the trees of righteousness the righteous will be in the Temple of Messiah.

One passage of the Gevurot reads, *"umatzmiach yeshua."* This is translated, "And makes Salvation sprout." This is an interesting Name of God alluding to Yeshua as the Branch. Branch is *"tzmach."* To sprout, a verb, is *"matzmiach."* In this passage, we affirm that Yeshua (Salvation) is the Branch promised, and the Power of Adonai's Salvation, Yeshua, will sprout all over the earth. This benediction praises Adonai for three types of resurrection: our daily awakening in Torah, life-restoring rain of blessing that causes seed to sprout, and the resurrection of the dead. Other Names of God are *Mechayeh Metim* (Resurrector of the Dead) and *Baal Gevurot* (Lord of Power).

---

70. Isaiah 61:1-4.

71. George M. Lamsa, Idioms in the Bible Explained and a Key to the Original Gospel, (San Francisco: HarperSanFransciso, 1985), 10.

72. I John 3:2.

CHAPTER NINE

Kedushot
Holiness

You are Holy, and Your Name is Holy, and holy ones praise you every day for eternity, for You are God, the Great and Holy King. Blessed are You, Adonai, the Holy God.

The Kedushot alludes to the patriarch Jacob, or Israel. One meaning of holy is "set apart." Jacob was set apart from his brother Esau by his holiness choices, such as his choice of wives to give birth to the twelve tribes. Holiness is the ability to influence one's environment and not to be affected by unholy influences. It is to be a non-conformist, refusing to live a lifestyle alien from Torah. On the other hand, one cannot withdraw completely from the world in the pursuit of holiness. The ultimate holiness is to be completely involved in daily life, and yet remain independent and unstained by it. This allows us to motivate everyone around us to reach higher levels of holiness. By obedience to God's Word, we create holy spaces no matter where we are.

The prayer says that "holy ones praise your name every day." This is not an arrogant prayer, for we are echoing Adonai's will as He states: *"You shall be holy, for I am holy."*[73]

---

73. Leviticus 19:2.

Our Father seeks holiness partners who work not for rewards, not for the esteem of men, but for the simple reason that we are to be holy because He is, and that is what He desires of us, just as an earthly father is delighted to see a son or daughter imitate him . This benediction confirms that by our conduct, one either sanctifies the Name and keeps it Holy, or profanes it. Names of God in this prayer are *Kadosh*, The Holy One, and *HaEl HaKadosh*, The Holy God.

Those who are partners with Adonai can avail much, because a holy one knows how to pray according to His will. Adonai upholds the fallen and heals the sick. One who prays this prayer becomes a holiness partner with Adonai, and he also has the commission to uphold the fallen and heal the sick. It is no accident that rabbis are ordained (*s'mikha*), which comes from the same root *somekh*, meaning "to lean," or to prop up, because it is a minister's job to support the falling and heal the sick with their righteous prayers. Striving for holiness with the Holy One is a powerful ministry principle, for true holy ones assist Yeshua in the repair of the Creation by making everything around them better: happier, healthier, and wiser.

Understanding holiness is the dominant theme of Leviticus, the Book of Purities. Since Christianity separated from Judaism, it has often been a neglected book, for many assume that since Yeshua died for our sins and there is no longer a physical Temple, then there is no need to make sense of it. It is, however, the most powerful and necessary book to teach how to fulfill the commandments of Acts 15 incumbent upon every non-Jewish believer: abstain from food polluted by idols, abstain from blood, abstain from strangled meats, and abstain from sexual immorality.

Leviticus reminds Israel that "the life is in the blood," whether of a human being or an animal. It is a holy thing, set apart, and there are very clear instructions on how life blood is to be handled, especially in meats Israel prepares for its own consumption. Israel's food is holy, different from the nations, because it is a holy people. It is a nation of priests, and likewise, every believer joined to Yeshua in covenant according to Ephesians 2 is a citizen of Israel and called to a holy table. For an Israelite to willfully disobey the commandment to handle all life blood carefully is to ignore the call to holy living. Even science bears out the wisdom of the holy diet. The most volatile diseases are transmitted through blood-borne pathogens and body fluids, whether from human to human or from animal to human. God's Word is our life and health if one obeys it.

There is also teaching in Leviticus about death blood. These are discharges of blood or body fluids, such as menstrual blood or abnormal penile discharge. Such blood or discharge is different from life blood because it is a result of tissue death or sickness. When an Israelite experiences these discharges, he or she enters a state of ritual uncleanness, or *tamei*, in Hebrew. This does not mean the person is dirty! For the woman, the monthly period is completely normal, and she is not to be seen as repulsive, but as holy! Holiness is separation from the ordinary. For the seven days of her period, a woman is in a heightened state of holiness, or separation from her husband. They are forbidden intimate contact during this period. Her husband must relate to her in a completely different way during this week. He must communicate with her mind, not her body, while she undergoes the cleansing process. The husband must respect her intellect, and that aspect of their relationship grows each month. It is part of the human psyche that what is forbidden to us, we desire. When a husband and wife observe the Levitical commandment to separate during the monthly period, the result is that his desire for her is greatly increased and their sexual and intellectual relationship improves over time instead of becoming mundane. Statistics prove this. Statistics also prove that couples who observe the Torah of *niddah*, or separation unto holiness, during the monthly period, reflect lower rates of cervical cancer.

There are other reasons to observe the instructions of holiness. Typically the woman's monthly period is considered to last seven days, "*And when a woman has a discharge, and the discharge from her flesh is blood, she has to be in her separation for seven days. And whoever touches her is unclean until evening. And whatever she lies on during her separation is unclean...*"[74] Again, this does not mean she is dirty! Something very important is happening between the holy couple and the Holy One. During this time of separation, the woman may not enter the precincts of the Tabernacle, and if her husband has relations with her during *niddah*, neither can he. This is an incredible picture of our redemption in Yeshua.

When one considers the first "unclean" thing in the creation, it was a fruit. It was the world's first non-kosher food. When this forbidden fruit was eaten, the Creation tumbled into a world of death, pain, and suffering. It was cursed to endure a week ("a day with the Lord is as a thousand years, and a thousand years as a day") of separation from the most intimate Presence of the Holy One. Adam and Eve, however, are promised a Redeemer who will restore the Creation. This Redeemer is the person Yeshua the Messiah. The Creation has now endured approximately six of the seven days of separation from the Presence of Holiness. Yeshua will soon return to set up a thousand-year Kingdom on Earth to finish the repair. It is a time when the Torah will go forth from Zion and the Word of the Lord from Jerusalem. This washing of water by the Word is symbolized by the woman's immersion in water following her *niddah*, according to Leviticus 15. When Yeshua's reign is completed on Earth, the world will be transformed and elevated to its original status as a place of peace, obedience, life, and blessing. For those who are in Him, over them death will have no power.

Women and men are given the responsibility to teach this process. By separating herself to holiness for seven days, the

---

74. Leviticus 15:19

wife teaches that the Earth is in a seven-year cleansing process. While it is in a state of separation from the most intimate Presence of the Holy One, the Earth is preparing itself for the re-unification and transformation of the Eighth Day, the New Jerusalem merging with Jerusalem, the spotless bride of Messiah Yeshua. By participating in the commandments of *niddah*, the holy woman participates in the redemption of Israel as a partner not only with her husband, but with her Bridegroom Yeshua. Although the husband and wife live in the same house during this seven-day period, they do not physically unite. Likewise, while the Creation endures this seven-day cleansing period, the Holy One dwells in us, for we are the Temples of the Holy Spirit. However, we do not yet enjoy the intimacy of full restoration. We are together yet not together. This is the Torah of blood separation.

It is also interesting that the husband may also be required to undergo a menstrual period according to Leviticus 15:24 if he is disobedient. *"And if any man lies with her at all, and her monthly flow is on him, he shall be unclean seven days. And any bed he lies on is unclean."* Although he has no blood flow, a man's disobedience in being intimate with his wife during her period causes him to be separated from the Tabernacle of the Presence for seven days as well. This is a picture of Adam's disobedience in also consuming the fruit. While it was not unclean to him as long as he was obedient to the commandment and remained separated from the fruit, it became an unclean thing when he was disobedient. Because they sinned together, both Adam and Eve suffered the separation together. Both men and women of the Earth are still living in Adam and Eve's *niddah* from intimacy with the Holy One. Until Yeshua returns to complete the cleansing process in His Kingdom, may we faithfully testify to the power of holiness, which is obedience to His teaching and instruction.

CHAPTER TEN

Daat
Knowledge

You kindly give man the gift of knowledge, and teach wisdom to frail man. Give with grace from Yourself with wisdom, insight, and knowledge. Blessed are You, Adonai, the gracious Giver of Knowledge.

The number of Hebrew words in the request for knowledge is seventeen, which is the numerical value of *tov,* good. These seventeen words correspond with the seventeen-word verse from Exodus 28:3 which reads, "*And you shall speak to all those who are wise hearted, whom I have filled with a spirit of wisdom...*" The number of letters in the blessing is sixty-eight, the numerical value of the Hebrew word *chaim,* or "life." Additionally, the blessing starts with the first Hebrew letter *alef* א and ends with the final Hebrew letter *tav* ת, suggesting that anyone with intellect and wisdom has everything. When Yeshua tells His sheep that He is the alpha and omega, in Hebrew he is saying he is the *alef* and the *tav.* He is the beginning and end of all wisdom, and if we have him, we have everything. The middle letter of the Hebrew alphabet is *mem* מ. The first, middle, and final letters of the Hebrew alphabet, *alef-mem-tav,* spell the word *emet* אמת, which is truth. Messiah Yeshua assures his disciples that He is The Way, The Truth (*emet*), and The Life (*chaim*).

This is the fourth blessing, which alludes to the fourth letter of the Hebrew alphabet, the *dalet*, which has the shape and meaning of an open doorway (ד). It is The Way to the Kingdom. It is also related to the word *dal*, a pauper, who hopefully knocks on doors begging for charity. The *dal* represents the poor in spirit. The ultimate goal of knowledge is to admit that we know nothing, and in this prayer, the petitioner assumes the role of a spiritual pauper who begs like Lazarus at the doorway of the rich man. With Yeshua, however, The Door is open and the Rich Man is faithful to meet our needs from His own table.

"Etz Yosef notes that the petition for wisdom is placed after the Holiness benediction, for we request only the wisdom and knowledge of what is holy."[75] Divine Wisdom is seen as equal to the *Ruach HaKodesh* according to Rashi, one of the greatest Jewish Bible commentators.[76] This may explain why Yeshua breathed on the disciples, and said, "*Receive the Ruach HaKodesh.*" Yeshua's action confirms Proverbs 2:6, which states: "*For Adonai gives wisdom; from His mouth come intellect and insight.*" This verse is not a casual arrangement of ideas. Wisdom/*chochmah* is to be desired, for it is given by Adonai. *Binah* and *daat*, or insight and knowledge, however, come from His mouth specifically. Moses died by the command (literally "the mouth") of Adonai. Therefore, one must have a strong bond to the Father to benefit from knowledge and insight, for it comes straight from His mouth. James said, "*If any man lack wisdom, let him ask of God, who gives to all men liberally.*" Wisdom, the basic raw material which results from the fear of Heaven, is given liberally. *Binah* and *daat* are the result of a closer walk with the Father. He kisses one on the mouth to breathe in his knowledge and discernment. *Chochmah* is the beginning, but it is also the end to those ever

---

75. Rabbi Avrohom Chaim Feuer, *Shemoneh Esrei*, (New York: Mesorah, 1990), 98.

76. Ibid.

seeking. The end of wisdom is *daat*, but once a Word of Torah is acquired, it initiates another cycle of development: wisdom, insight, and knowledge.

The second step toward *daat* is *binah*, or insight. The word is related to *binyan*, which is structure, or building. As one delves into the details of Torah, whether a statute, a commandment, or an ordinance, he perceives the underlying design and structure of that Word. *Binah* is a process of deepening and broadening one's comprehension. It is the ability to make connections with smaller precepts and to fit them into the larger redemptive plan for the universe.

One characteristic of *daat* is intellectual strength; it is the courage of strong convictions and opinions not easily shaken. The supplicant may learn a new commandment or a word of Torah, but at first, he is timid. He may not want others to see him practicing it, because he's not sure he convincingly can explain why he's doing it. This is simply wisdom based upon reverence for God's Word, and there is merit in it. However, as one continues practicing the commandment, it becomes a habit, and he understands more as he walks in it, so he acquires confidence in his commandment. He has allowed it to become a living word in him, and he has imitated his Messiah Yeshua, The Living Word. He has become a living, breathing Scripture. This is *daat*, spiritual insight. The *Ruach HaKodesh's* kiss of breath brings the commandment to life. Some commandments come to life easily, but some are resurrected out of the dead flesh slowly. Once this Word of Torah is acquired, though, it is a strong conviction of intellectual strength, not just blind faith. The Name of God in this benediction is *Chonen HaDaat*, Giver of Knowledge.

CHAPTER ELEVEN

Teshuvah
Repentance

Cause us to return, Our Father, to Your Torah, and draw us near, our King, to Your service, and cause us to return in perfect repentance before You. Blessed are You, Adonai, Who desires repentance.

Teshuvah is a request for the Father to accept repentance from sin. It is the fifth benediction, or the number five, which is *heh* (ה). The structure of the ה has a disconnected foot on the left-hand side with a small gap in the letter's top near the roof, or horizontal bar forming the top of the *heh*. This signifies that a space always remains open through which a repentant sinner can return and be drawn in to the Father's House.[77] There is an old chassidic tale that tells of a father whose son turned his back on him and God. He went far away, and lived in sin and darkness. The father sent a message to the son to return to him. The son said, "I cannot return to your house." The father sent a message back, "Come as far as you can, and I will meet you."[78]

---

77. Michael Munk, *Wisdom in the Hebrew Alphabet*, (New York: Mesorah Publications, Ltd., 1983), 87.

78. Chaim Potok, The Chosen, (Twentieth Century Fox Corporation: 1982).

If one feels that it is beyond his power to return to the Torah, the Father says, "Return as far as you can, and I will meet you." He will take the responsibility to meet the one who repents, and to slowly lead him back to His House and His Torah. This is the whole message of Galatians: a Gentile should come as far as he knows how and let the Holy Spirit lead him into the commandments slowly. He should not depend upon works of the law for his salvation, but faith in Yeshua's perfect work. Keeping the commandments are outworkings of salvation. The Galatians were no different than many new believers today. Some thought the words of the Torah were interesting Jewish tales with some value lessons, but they'd had no informed instruction in Torah as the oracles of God established by grace. Others believed their salvation was earned or guaranteed by keeping a selected part of the Scriptures as interpreted by their denomination's doctrines; in the case of the Galatians, they believed circumcision was necessary for salvation. Abraham, however, even after the covenant was made, spent many years learning Adonai's statutes and commandments before he was circumcised. He continued to walk in faith and obey what he understood until the time was revealed to him by Adonai.

Each believer has different needs, and the Holy Spirit will reveal the oracles of God to him at the appropriate time if the believer is willing to read the Word, pray, and then not harden his heart. Although Rabbi Shaul urged believers to run the race as one who wants to win the prize, most days it is a walk, not a dead run! If you feel as though you're running too fast to sustain the course, it may be the result of listening to those who are trying to impose manmade commandments or even the commandments of God out of their proper time. The "Judaizers" of Galatians were trying to impose circumcision, a valid commandment for a native-born Israelite who would be reared in a love and respect for the Word, onto newly-converted pagans, who had no idea how to act. They were not reared in a home of respect for the Torah, one

Supreme God, or His covenant people. They would make many mistakes as they learned the Living Word, and those mistakes might bring reproach on the community of faith. Were they still attending pagan feasts? Were they still disrespecting father and mother or stealing? Circumcision certainly was not the answer to their level of understanding. However, if after they came to a full understanding of the covenants and began to walk a redeemed path that did not bring constant reproach to Yeshua's name, then like Timothy, they may take a step of circumcision. The question of circumcision is an ancient rabbinic argument. Some rabbis believed that a convert should be immediately circumcised. Others believed as Rabbi Shaul did, that circumcision should only occur after the convert had gained enough insight and knowledge to walk in the more important commandments without bringing reproach to the community.

The Torah has been equated with bondage to manmade and imposed regulations, not the simple graceful Torah practiced and taught by Yeshua, who neither added to nor took away from his Father's Torah. Sometimes our repentance should include turning away from doctrines that add to or take away from our Father's Torah, and particularly should we repent of "works of the law," those commandments with which we try to earn our salvation or keep it. The Torah came through Moses; grace and truth came through Yeshua. Salvation and repentance are in the turning back to the Father. Quality of life and reward are in the faith walk back to His home.

In this blessing, God is Father, just as Yeshua taught. Furthermore, the *heh* ה is the number of the five books of Torah, which teach a repentant sinner how to return to the Father. The benediction begins with a *heh* and ends with a *heh*, so it begins with repentance and ends with repentance, and if one adds five and five, the sum is ten, which equals the Ten Awesome Days of Repentance before Yom Kippur and the Ten Commandments. The Name of God in this benediction is *HaRotzeh Bitshuvah*, Desirer of Repentance.

There is a point to praying for "perfect repentance," not just repentance. If Adonai is a Father, then the child should not repent out of self-preservation or fear of punishment. Many people serve God out of fear of hellfire. This is imperfect, because it is only self-preservation. Perfect repentance is repentance motivated by love, and it desires to make God alone the focal point of life. It is a desire to seek God and to be joined with Him.

CHAPTER TWELVE

Slichah
Forgiveness

Forgive us, our Father, for we have made errors; pardon us, our King, for we have sinned willfully, for You are a Good and forgiving God. Blessed are You, Adonai, Gracious One, Who forgives abundantly.

The Scriptural foundation for this request in its order after the prayer of Teshuvah is found in Isaiah 55:7: "*Let the wicked forsake his way, and the man of crime, his schemes; and let each repent unto Adonai, and He will have mercy upon him, and unto our God, for He will abundantly forgive.*" According to this Scripture, the first step is to forsake the sin, to repent and turn back to the Torah, and then Adonai will forgive abundantly. Before Yeshua ever tells one sinner, "*Thy sins be forgiven thee,*" John the Baptist commands people everywhere to repent. Repentance precedes and prepares the way for forgiveness.

"Forgive us our Father, for we have made errors." Forgiveness for errors is as necessary as forgiveness for willful sin. The less one knows of Torah, the more likely he is to err, for Yeshua says, "*You do greatly err, not knowing the Scriptures.*" "*Forgive them, Father, for they don't know what they're doing.*"[79]

---

79. Luke 23:34.

Errors are unintentional. This prayer petitions the Father to overlook blunders as His children become aware of what sin is through studying His Word. Once aware, though, Yeshua expects obedience, "*If you were blind you would have no sin,*" Yeshua replied, "*but since you say, 'We see' your sin remains.*"[80] Furthermore, *if we sin willfully after having come to a knowledge of truth, then what sacrifice remains for sin?*[81]

In Psalm 51 are the principles of repentance. David laments, "*For I recognize my willful sins; and my error is before me always.*" David is mourning for the sins he has committed willfully. His errors, the lighter sins, are always before him as well. What rabbis say this means is that it is the lighter sins that lead to the serious willful sins of adultery, deceit, and manslaughter. David knows that the Torah commands that a king is not to multiply wives to himself; nevertheless, he collects more than a modest number of wives and fails to properly monitor his children, which results in incest, rape, and murder in his own house.

Forgiveness in the Slichah is relative to the wave offering described in the Torah, which is the breast of the animal. Remember the publican? A publican is a tax collector. This tax collector is so repentant, so meek, so humble before his Father, he can't even look up toward Heaven; he merely looks down, beats his breast, and pleads for mercy. It is this very kind of humility before Adonai that will cause us to ascend the heights of holiness.

> He spoke also this parable to certain people who were convinced of their own righteousness, and who despised all others. "Two men went up into the temple to pray; one was a Parush (Pharisee), and the other was a tax collector. The Parush stood and prayed to himself like this: 'God, I thank you, that I

---

80. John 9:41.
81. Hebrews 10:26.

am not like the rest of men, extortioners, unright-
eous, adulterers, or even like this tax collector. I fast
twice a week. I give tithes of all that I get.' But the
tax collector, <u>standing far away</u>, wouldn't even lift up
his eyes to heaven, but beat his breast, saying, 'God,
be merciful to me, <u>a sinner</u>!' I tell you, this man
went down to his house justified rather than the
other; for everyone who exalts <u>himself</u> will be hum-
bled, but he who humbles <u>himself</u> will be exalted."[82]

The two men have come to the Temple to pray, so they
have have brought an animal, grain, or money offering. In
Hebrew, an offering is a *korban*, which is accompanied in
Second Temple times by prayer. The Pharisee thanks Adonai
that he is not like other sinful men, and waves his own
works of self-righteousness as an offering under Adonai's
nose, which was not a sweet-smelling aroma of repentance.
Talk about "works of the law"! Ironically, this Pharisee was
everything he said he wasn't. He had merely built a religious
kingdom to himself that was exactly like the man-made
kingdoms of unfair taxation and adulterous practices he
condemned. Although Yeshua's teachings agreed about 80
percent of the time with the School of Hillel Pharisees, in
the issue of divorce, the Hillel Pharisees twisted the Torah to
legitimize divorce practices that Yeshua said were adultery!
The religious elite had also legitimized a practice of making
goods or money "*korban*," or dedicated to the Temple. The
person could dedicate the money, or make it *herem*, but still
continue to control or invest it in his lifetime. A *korban* is
the generic term of a Temple offering. Yeshua reproves these
greedy men who made their money *korban* to the Temple so
that they wouldn't have the burden of supporting elderly
parents. Did they really think that a man-made law could
set aside their responsibility to honor their fathers and

---

82. Luke 18:9

mothers? "Then some Pharisees and scribes came to Jesus from Jerusalem and said,

"Why do Your disciples break the tradition of the elders?

For they do not wash their hands when they eat bread." And He answered and said to them, "Why do you yourselves transgress the commandment of God for the sake of your tradition? "For God said, 'HONOR YOUR FATHER AND MOTHER,' and, 'HE WHO SPEAKS EVIL OF FATHER OR MOTHER IS TO BE PUT TO DEATH.' "But you say, 'Whoever says to his father or mother, "Whatever I have that would help you has been given to God," he is not to honor his father or his mother.' And by this you invalidated the word of God for the sake of your tradition."[83]

Calling this dedicated money an offering did not make it acceptable for the altar. A disciple of Yeshua can't steal the money that rightfully belongs to family support, use it himself, then try to bribe Adonai's acceptance by pinning a religious name on it. This proud Pharisee was everything he said he wasn't in his prayer, and then he refused to repent! Where there is no repentance, there can be no forgiveness.

Rather, the tax collector acknowledges his sin and repents humbly. He doesn't pretend he is righteous. He beats his breast, the portion of the wave offering. He offers his heart of repentance to Adonai, while not even feeling worthy to lift his eyes heavenward or to draw near, which is what an offering is, a *korban*, the Hebrew word for drawing near. His humility in bringing his *korban* of repentant prayer is what causes him to ascend to a height of acceptance that the self-made kingdom man, the Pharisee, could not. Traditions that prevent us from keeping the simple Torah of God make us no holier and no

---

83. Matthew 15:1-9

more accepted than the worst sinner who turns from his ways in repentance; in fact, the Father rejects our traditions and chooses the humble one who has turned from his own way back to the Father. The publican has humility with repentance, and he acknowledges his sin that prevents him from fulfilling his Kingdom commission as an Israelite. The Pharisee is elevated in his own religious kingdom by arrogance and pseudo-commandments, but the tax collector is elevated in Adonai's Kingdom and drawn near to His Glory by humility.

To this day, when Jews pray the Slichah, it is customary to strike one's chest with the fist to demonstrate outwardly the repentance of the heart. Adonai knows whether we offer the breast of the wave offering with repentance or pride. Since the heart is where sin originates, striking the chest is like knocking on the heart's door to awaken the sleeper of denial within. The Slichah is the Hebrew way of saying, "Excuse me." The Names of God are "Gracious One," or "*Chanun*," and "One Who Forgives Abundantly," "*HaMarbeh Leesloach.*"

CHAPTER THIRTEEN

Geulah
Redemption

*Notice, please, our affliction, take up our grievance, and
quickly redeem us with a full redemption for the sake of Your
Name, for You are God the Mighty Redeemer. Blessed are You,
Adonai, Redeemer of Israel.*

The prayer for redemption asks Adonai to notice affliction and grief. Cures for ills of the spirit precede healing
for the ailments of the body. The Father recognizes His children's pain, just as He hears Leah's prayer of anguish because
she is unloved. Leah is rewarded with a son whom she names
Reuben, and she says, *"for Adonai has observed my affliction."*[84] Adonai is also very interested in redeeming Israel not
only for the sake of relieving her suffering, but for the sake of
His Name. The prayer requests a speedy redemption for His
Name's sake.

This benediction is number seven, which is the letter
zayin in Hebrew. It speaks of Messiah and the seven years of
Messiah's travail. The world will teeter on the brink of destruc-
tion before it enters the era of unsurpassed serenity and peace.
The letter *zayin* also means "weapon," so this petition requests

---

84. Genesis 29:32.

that Adonai fight Israel's battles, and that no weapon formed against her will prosper. Notice the wording, "take up our grievance." During the times of testing, Adonai's children are not alone, but part of a community, and His children pray for speedy redemption and deliverance as part of the Body of Messiah. The Name of God invoked in this benediction is *Goel Yisrael*, Redeemer of Israel.

CHAPTER FOURTEEN

Rephuah
Health and Healing

Heal us, Adonai, and we will be healed, save us, and we will be saved, for You are our Praise. Bring cure and healing for all our sicknesses, sufferings, and ailments, for You are God and King, a faithful and compassionate Healer. Blessed are You, Adonai, Healer of the sick of His people Israel.

The text of the prayer is based upon Jeremiah 17:14: *"Heal me, Adonai, then I shall be healed; save me—then I shall be saved, for You are my praise."* This is a request for divine healing, not the incomplete healing attempted by human doctors or medicines. When a human doctor intervenes, he often treats only the symptoms, so the pain may return when the medicine is withdrawn. This prayer is for complete healing of the underlying ailment, not just temporary relief. It is also considered a prayer for immunity from future sickness.

The Hebrew word for a sick person, *choleh*, is cognate with the word *chol*, which means unholy or profane. The term *chol* is related to the word *chalal*, vacuum; emptiness. Where there is a void of sanctity, physical debilitation and illness may ensue. The Hebrew word for health, *briot*, is cognate with *bria*, creation, implying that a person is healthy when he lives up to what God created him to be.[85] There are other explanations for illness, but Yeshua sometimes makes a connection between sin and sickness.[86] The Apostle James also teaches this connection, for in his instructions to the scattered twelve tribes, he says in chapter 5 of his epistle, *"Is anyone among you sick? He must call for the elders of the church and they are to pray over him, anointing him with oil in the name of the Lord; and the prayer offered in faith will restore the one who is sick, and the Lord will raise him up, and if he has committed sins, they will be forgiven him. Therefore, confess your sins to one another, and pray for one another so that you may be healed."* The Psalms also indicate that poor health may sometimes be the result of sin: *"There is no soundness in my flesh because of Your anger, Nor any health in my bones because of my sin."*[87]

There are twenty-seven words in this eighth blessing. There are also twenty-seven letters in Proverbs 4:22: *"For they [words of Torah] are life to those who find them, and a healing to all their flesh."* There are twenty-seven total letters in the Hebrew alphabet with which that Torah is written. The Words of Torah are life, for our *Ropheh* sends His Word to heal us. If the petitioner is sin-sick, there are Words of healing for him, for the Healer is more merciful than any doctor. He has given us the oldest medical manual in the universe. When we pray for the sick in this benediction, it is customary to insert special prayers for the sick and to call them specifically by name. The Names of God in this blessing are *Ropheh Choleh*, Healer of the Sick, and *Tehillatenu*, Our Praise.

---

85. Feuer, 135.
86. John 5:14.
87. Psalm 38:3

CHAPTER FIFTEEN

Beerkhat Hashanim
The Prosperous Year

*Bless for us, Adonai our God, this year and all types of crops
for good, and give dew and rain for blessing on the face of the
earth, and satisfy us from its goodness, and bless our year like
the best years for blessing. For You are the good and giving
God Who blesses the years. Blessed are You, Adonai, Who
blesses the years.*

It is not wrong to pray for prosperity in the proper perspective. The Father does not so much care if His children have
nice cars, big homes, or a big raise. According to Yeshua's
parables, what He does care about is whether we dedicate all
of our increase to the Kingdom. Does the supplicant see his
financial assets as simply goods he invests for the Landlord of
Creation, and does he act as though the Landlord will sit
down and demand to see the ledgers when He returns? Any
other view is embezzlement from the Kingdom of Heaven. In
whatever one prospers, it is merely sustenance to enable the
performance of God's will and to testify of His Kingdom. The
writer of the Epistles of John, which are strongly pro-Torah,
assures the Body, *"Beloved, I pray that you prosper in all things,
even as your soul prospers."*[88]

---

88. 3 John 1:2

The benediction is placed in the ninth position because it corresponds to Psalm 9. The Psalm in modern Bibles is 10, but in ancient times, Psalms 1 and 2 were one chapter, so the original number of Psalm 10 is Psalm 9.[89] In this Psalm, David condemns the greedy merchants who drive up food prices and make huge profits at the expense of the poor. This is the lowest form of greed because the poor have no defense or choice against high food prices.

The ninth benediction serves as more than a reminder of the proper reasons to ask for prosperity. The ninth letter of the *alefbet* is *tet*, and tet is the first letter of *tov*, goodness. In the days of the Creation, Elohim saw that His Creation was "good," or "*tov*." With this blessing, one asks the Father to share with His children all the goodness that was present in the *tov* Creation. With this prayer, we are also reminded that the Second Adam is in the process of restoring the Creation to its original good condition. This blessing is a corporate prayer for the "face of the Earth," and for all to benefit from the blessing, not just the personal community of the petitioner. In the Earth before sin, there was no rain, only a mist that rose up from the deep of the earth to water the living things. Remember, in Hebraic thought, rain is truth from Heaven. In a perfect Creation, God's truth simply rises and permeates all areas of life. The dew is the distillation of that truth; it is God's Word becoming clear to us, and the dew, like a precious gem, glitters in the light of the sun. In Adam's world, God's Truth was evident in all things, and beautiful every morning. In a fallen world, we must wait for the rain from Heaven, and we must pray for either rain or dew each day. When Messiah Yeshua returns, may He rain his Truth on all the earth, and may it distill like the dew in our minds and hearts.

This benediction for prosperity recalls Yeshua's temptation on the pinnacle of the Temple. It is presumptuous to

89. Feuer, 142.

76

spend money to satisfy more than practical needs, and then to expect Adonai to ease that burden. Yeshua could have unnecessarily leaped from the heights and requested angels to catch Him, but He replies, *"Thou shalt not tempt the Lord thy God."* Neither should a believer throw himself from a financial pinnacle and expect to be rescued. Those who speculate on highly risky business transactions, such as junk bonds, are usually motivated by greed, not hunger. It is the same with those who faithfully buy lottery tickets and pray to Adonai that their number will win. Often these people say that if they win the lottery, they will give thousands of dollars to church or charity. The desire to give to charity is rarely their motivation in buying the ticket or praying for its success. In fact, the truth behind such a prayer is that once the winnings have first satisfied the petitioner's covetousness, he will give the leftovers or a commission to God. What a deal. The Apostle James says that such prayers are not answered because they are "consumed upon your lust."

This prayer is a reminder to be satisfied with Adonai's idea of bounty. This does not excuse one from working hard at jobs or businesses, but it does relieve one of the responsibility to be a huge success. *"The bounty of Adonai truly enriches, and He adds no sorrow to it."*[90] The righteous does his best at work, dedicates the firstfruits to the Kingdom, then his share of that fruit satisfies because it is the Master's expert will. Some years the blessing is mighty: *"And Isaac planted in that land and received in that year a hundredfold, for Adonai blessed him."*[91]

There are other forms of prosperity than financial and physical. There is also such a thing as spiritual prosperity. Since this prayer is ninth in order, there is an allusion to a pregnancy come to term. Many believers pray for blessings that require forces to move in spiritual and emotional realms.

---

90. Proverbs 10:22.
91. Bereishit 26:12

One believer may pray for her family to find a relationship with Messiah Yeshua. Another may pray for a call to ministry to be realized. Some may pray for release from a job that constantly tests their faith in Adonai. This prayer reminds believers that many blessings do not come instantly, or even quickly.

Some blessings are brought forth from the secret places of the earth, like the blessing of conception. Spiritual blessings must gestate according to a Divine timetable, just as every new birth. A woman who is six months pregnant does not complain that her baby cannot walk or solve algebra problems. These milestones are attained in their proper times. Often when prayers are not answered, it is because there is a Divine timetable, so one must not be impatient during their gestation. Have at least as much faith in the spiritual gestation of prayers as in the physical gestation of a baby!

It is a Kingdom goal to give birth to many spiritual children; therefore, a disciple of Yeshua may be sitting on many spiritual "eggs" at one time. If impatience with that process sets in, then one may be tempted to run off and leave the egg before it hatches. The egg will not hatch until it is time, but it certainly will not hatch if it is abandoned. Many who follow Yeshua have not let patience have her perfect work, and they run from church to church or ministry to ministry seeking instant birth to their spiritual vision or prayers. They may be laying eggs all over town, yet none of them ever hatch! The pastors, friends, and families of these impatient chickens wish that they would stop, be patient, be consistent, be faithful, and sit on just one good spiritual egg. Patience is what gives birth to sustainable spiritual vision because the faithful disciple will wait until patience has prepared its perfect work.

By requesting the rain and dew at its proper time in the Beerkhat HaShanim, a disciple requests Divine timing in when and how much moisture falls on the earth or in his life. In Israel, if the rain falls at an improper time, it destroys the crops. There are times when only dew is the right amount of moisture. The early and latter rain in their proper times is the Divine yearly cycle in the Holy Land to bring forth the harvest. One should remember in praying this benediction that we want our financial, physical, and spiritual blessings to arrive at the right time and in the right amounts to maximize our harvest in the Kingdom of Heaven.

The Name of God in this blessing is *Adonai Mevarekh Hashanim*, God Who Blesses the Years.

CHAPTER SIXTEEN

Keebutz Gahluyot
Ingathering of Exiles

Blow the great (trumpet) shofar for our freedom, raise the banner to gather our exiles and quickly gather us from the four corners of the earth to our Land. Blessed are You, Adonai, Who gathers in His scattered people Israel.

There are two types of exiles: the outcasts of Israel, and the dispersed of Judah,[92] who return from the four corners of the earth. According to Isaiah 27:13, these exiles will be gathered at the blasting sound of the great *shofar*. A *shofar* is a ram's horn. The two horns of the ram sacrificed in place of Isaac are symbolic in rabbinic literature. The left horn is said to have been sounded at the giving of the Torah at Sinai. The right horn, which was larger, and is known as the "great shofar," will be sounded by Adonai Himself when the time comes to redeem the exiles of Israel.

Now that the firstfruits of Judah have returned to the Holy Land to bring forth fruit on the mountains of the Golan and Ephraim, we understand Ezekiel 36:8: "*You mountains of Israel, sprout your branches and give forth your fruit to My people Israel, for they are close to returning.*" The

---

92. Isaiah 11:11-12.

sprouting and fruiting of the Israeli mountains is not a sign that all have returned, but they are close to returning. The Talmud says two types of people can be called children of Zion: the person who was actually born there, and the one who always yearned to live there.[93] While reciting this benediction, it is very important to tune into the yearning of the heart to live in Israel. According to many sages in the Mishnah and Talmud,[94] even the ten lost tribes who seem to have disappeared forever will return to Israel. The King constantly reaches out to those who seem to have dropped from the ranks of Israel. *"The Lord does not take away life, rather He devises means to prevent the abandoned from remaining abandoned."*[95] King David said, *"I have strayed like a lost sheep—seek out Your servant."* Not only does the King devise ways to gather the abandoned, King David demonstrates that the sheep must acknowledge that they've strayed and ask to be found.

There will be a gathering of lost sheep at the sound of the great shofar. They will acknowledge that they've strayed, yearn for their Land, yearn for their Torah given to the sound of the shofar, and become one People, *yachad.* "And gather us together" in Hebrew is, *"Vehkabtzenu yachad."* This is more than a request for physical unity; it is a request for spiritual unity so that Israel can dwell together: *"Hineh mah tov umah naim, shevet achim gam yachad,"* "Behold how good and how pleasant it is for brothers to dwell together in unity."

This benediction is tenth. The word for collection, *kibbutz* is in the title, *"Kibbutz Galuyot."* The *galut* is the dispersion of Israel into the nations of the earth. A kibbutz is a collective farm or community in Israel, or a gathering of people. This gathering of people is tenth in sequence because it is appropriate to pray for a regathering with the number of a *minyan,*

---

93. Kesubos 75a.
94. Sanhedrin 110b.
95. 2 Samuel 14:14.

the minimum number for community prayer. One reason that ten is the precise minimum for public prayer is that Adonai called the ten faithless spies who returned from Canaan an "evil congregation." Another reason is the account of Abraham's plea for mercy when Sodom was to be destroyed. The minimum acceptable number of righteous men in a city was ten.

Another allusion to the number ten is found in Zechariah 8:23: *"Thus saith the LORD of hosts; In those days it shall come to pass, that ten men shall take hold out of all languages of the nations, even shall take hold of the skirt of him that is a Jew, saying, We will go with you: for we have heard that God is with you."* These ten men of the nations, a *minyan*, are asking to become *yachad*, or one, with the returning Jews, for they have heard that God is with the Jews and not against them. These ten men are also part of returning Israel, and have a portion in the Torah and the Land along with their Jewish brothers who return. How do we know that the non-Jew has a portion in the Holy Land?

> Isaiah 56:1-8 Thus says the LORD, "Preserve justice and do righteousness, For My **salvation** (Yeshua) is about to come And My righteousness to be revealed." "How blessed is the man who does this, and the son of man who takes hold of it; Who keeps from profaning the Sabbath, And keeps his hand from doing any evil." Let not the foreigner who has joined himself to the LORD say, "The LORD will surely separate me from His people." Nor let the eunuch say, "Behold, I am a dry tree." For thus says the LORD, "To the eunuchs who keep My sabbaths, And choose what pleases Me, And hold fast My covenant, To them I will give in My house and within My walls a memorial, And a name better than that of sons and daughters; I will give them an everlasting name which will not be cut off. "Also the **foreigners** who

join themselves to the LORD, To minister to Him, and to love the name of the LORD, To be His servants, every one who keeps from profaning the sabbath and holds fast My covenant; Even those I will bring to My holy mountain and make them joyful in My house of prayer. Their burnt offerings and their sacrifices will be acceptable on My altar; **For My house will be called a house of prayer for all the peoples.**" The Lord GOD, who **gathers the dispersed of Israel**, declares, "Yet {others} I will gather to them, to those {already} gathered."

This gathering, according to Rabbi Shapiro, the Munkatcher Rebbe, will be nothing other than a miracle, for it is impossible for it to take place through political or military means.[96] He derives this from the wording in Hebrew for "Raise the banner (*nes*) to gather our exiles." *Nes* means "banner." One of the Names of God is Adonai Nisi, or The Lord My Banner. To gather a group, one needs a rallying point, a place where all can collect to wait for instruction. This is what Yeshua is, the Living Torah, a banner under which both Jew and righteous Gentiles from the nations can collect and rally. *Nes* in Hebrew also means "miracle." So the rabbi translates the prayer, "Raise a miracle to gather our exiles." If the Jews are praying for a miraculous return, then it is incumbent upon all believers in Messiah Yeshua to pray for this miracle to take place according to the Scriptures. The Name of God mentioned is "*YHVH Mekabetz Needchei Amo Yisrael,*" the Lord Who Gathers His Dispersed People Israel."

Notice also that twice the passage from Isaiah cites Sabbath-keeping as a requisite for being included in the regathering of Israel and the gathering of the nations with them. Why is Sabbath-keeping such an important first step for the nations? The Sabbath is the remembrance of the

---

96. Feuer, 156.

Creation. The Messiah's mission was, is, and will be to restore the perfect Creation to the state that His Father made it: "good." To the living creatures of the Earth, man was the crown of Creation. For the work of Creation, the Sabbath Day was the crown. The commission of the Second Adam is to restore both man and all Creation to the "very good" state during His thousand-year Sabbath reign. The righteous and all creation will rest in King Yeshua's restorative work for a full Sabbath, a thousand years of peace and knowledge of the Most High.

To the children of Israel, the Sabbath was given as a "sign" of their covenant with Adonai, like a betrothal ring. One day the faithful bride will dine with the Groom at their marriage supper, but until then, she must remain faithful to the covenant. Keeping the Sabbath, our Lord, says, is a sign between us until that day. Should we remove our betrothal ring, the keeping of the Sabbath, we tell the world that we are not betrothed to Messiah, that He is not restoring all things according to His Divine Commission from the Father, and that we will not be prepared for the ultimate fulfillment of His work, which is the completion of the work. If we do not keep the Sabbath, then are we really betrothed? We, too, have a part in regaining the glory that existed in the perfect, good, and glorious Creation. Every Sabbath we keep is a sign and a prophecy of Messiah Yeshua's completed work of restoration. Talk about Abraham's faith!

CHAPTER SEVENTEEN

Din
Restoration of Justice

Restore our judges as in former times, and our counselors as at the beginning. Remove from us sorrow and groaning, and soon reign over us, You, Adonai, only, with kindness and compassion, and justify us in righteousness and judgment. Blessed are You Adonai, the King Who loves righteousness and judgment.

Benediction number eleven has a specific purpose for its placement. Eleven is the number of attributes that David says a righteous man displays, and these are attributes necessary for a righteous judge. This is found in Psalm 15:

> O LORD, who may abide in Your tent? Who may
> dwell on Your holy hill?
> He who walks with integrity and works righteous-
> ness,
> And speaks truth in his heart.
> He does not slander with his tongue,
> Nor does evil to his neighbor,
> Nor takes up a reproach against his friend;
> In whose eyes a reprobate is despised,
> But who honors those who fear the LORD;
> He swears to his own hurt and does not change;

He does not put out his money at interest,
Nor does he take a bribe against the innocent. He
who does these things will never be shaken.

These eleven critical attributes of honesty are what the King is looking for in a judge over His people. This prayer is for those in leadership over Israel. He or she translates the Torah into a practical application. The judge is given these powers of binding and loosing in order to bring order and justice to the Body of Messiah. This is not just a prayer for those who lead the Body of Messiah. Individuals have different gifts, but each area is important to the Body. Whatever one's area of anointing, gifting, or ministry, he or she should aspire to be a leader, and the needed qualities are these eleven from Psalm 15. Even ladies may function as judges, as Judge Deborah so well illustrated. However, a minister who must constantly compromise Scripture according to the will of the choir, deacon board, a committee, or the biggest tither, is a shaken judge, for he has neglected one or more of the eleven attributes of righteousness. A righteous judge should be fearless save the fear of Heaven. On a personal level, each believer should be fearless in judging himself. He must act according with the Scriptural ethics and values that he has judged as true and binding, and then enforce them upon himself as a righteous judge.

Active self-judgment is necessary because in Proverbs 29:4, it says, *"Through justice the king establishes the land; but he who stands aloof overthrows it."* It is the king's responsibility to establish justice with righteous judges, but anyone who stands aloof can overthrow this righteousness with apathy. One can be impartial in judgment, but he can never be impartial about judgment. All should be very interested in learning not only Adonai's judgments, but skill in how to apply them, beginning with one's self.

Having met the prerequisite of judging himself and others favorably, the prayer says, "justify us through judgment."

This petitions the Judge of all the earth for justification if the supplicant has judged others righteously. Yeshua taught the disciples, "*Forgive us our debts as we forgive our debtors*." This prayer is a good time to meditate upon misjudgment of others and the eleven attributes of a righteous judge. If we as judges see that we've misjudged, we may set our ways aright in this benediction.

The benediction closes with an acknowledgment, "Blessed are you, Adonai, the King who loves righteousness and judgment." It is difficult for this generation to understand this statement. When God is promoted among the lost or the backslider, He is usually given raving reviews in the areas of mercy, grace, forgiveness, and patience toward the sinner. These are all accurate attributes of Him, but unless these comforting attributes are balanced with a caution that Adonai loves justice, the promotion is inaccurate. Where does Scripture say that Adonai *loves* grace or mercy? Yes, He displays these attributes, and he desires them, but in Psalm 99, it is clear that "*Mighty is the King Who loves judgment*." He loves it!

The benediction for Din reminds us that Adonai Himself loves to establish righteous judgment among his people. In the messages from the Prophets to Israel, Adonai's greatest wrath against Judah and Israel was a result of dishonest judgment, not just idolatry. He has a special interest in Israel's fairness and responsibility toward one another, which may be summed up in Yeshua's words, "Love your neighbor as yourself." Justice ensures that we will respect our neighbor's right to grow and thrive in the Kingdom of Heaven. Psalm 82:1 states, "*God stands in the assembly of God; in the midst of the judges, He shall judge*." When judges meet, Adonai is very interested in evaluating the righteousness of their decisions and deliberations. According to rabbinic thought, if the judges are sincere, then Adonai will prevent them from being deceived by false witnesses. It is this way in which the Righteous Judge removes sorrow and groaning from the

Body of Messiah. The only groaning that should result from a righteous judgment is the groaning of dying flesh, which is the rejoicing of the spirit growing in Messiah. What flesh mourns over should cause the spirit to rejoice. The Talmud teaches that a righteous judge causes the Spirit of God to descend upon the entire congregation. Righteous judges within the Body of Messiah are a gift of love from the King Who Loves Righteousness and Judgment, *Melekh Ohev Tzedekah Umishpat.*

CHAPTER EIGHTEEN

HaMinim
Heretics

And may slanderers have no hope, and all the heretics die in a moment, and may all the enemies of your people be cut off speedily. May You quickly uproot, destroy, and throw down the sinners: destroy them, lower them, and humiliate them in our days. Blessed are You, Adonai, who breaks enemies and humbles sinners.

It is important to understand what the twelfth benediction is, but it should not be prayed by believers in Yeshua the Messiah. Again, DO NOT PRAY THIS PRAYER! It is only given for your understanding as to the origin of this benediction. The benediction in its present form is not the original, and was not part of the original prayers. The spirit of it is markedly different from the other benedictions. Here is the original reading of the prayer from the year 90 C.E.: "For the renegades let there be no hope, and may the arrogant kingdom soon be rooted out in our days, and the Nazarenes and the Minim perish as in a moment and be blotted out from the book of life."[97]

The *minim* is an acronym for believers in Yeshua. In Judaism, Yeshua is called *Yeshu*. His followers were called *Min*

---

97. Feuer. 177.

or *Notzrim*. The acronym is *mah-ah-mi-nay yeshu notzri*, which means "believers in Yeshu the Nazarene." This benediction was composed in 90 C.E. so that the Nazarenes could be discovered, for of course they would not pray a curse on themselves. In this way, they were identified, punished, or thrown out of the synagogues, just as Yeshua predicted. Many Nazarenes did not leave the synagogues voluntarily, but were kicked out by the heirs of the Pharisees. Lest one think too badly of the Jews, the Christian churches did the same to the Nazarenes or to anyone who ventured to keep the Mosaic law, the Torah.

This is the Christian counterpart of the benediction against the heretics, which is known as Constantine's Creed: "Constantine's Creed: As a preliminary to his acceptance as a catechumen, a Jew 'Must confess and denounce verbally, the whole of Hebrew people, forthwith declare that with a whole heart and sincere faith he desires to be received among the Christians. Then he must renounce openly in the church all Jewish superstition, the priest saying, and he, or his sponsor if he is a child, replying in these words:

> I renounce all customs, rites, legalisms, unleavened
> breads and sacrifices of the lambs of the Hebrews, all
> of the other feasts of the Hebrews, sacrifices, prayers,
> aspersions, purifications, sanctifications, propitia-
> tions, and fasts and new moons, and Sabbaths, and
> superstitions, and hymns and chants, and obser-
> vances of the synagogues, and the food and drink of
> the Hebrews; in one word, I now renounce
> absolutely everything Jewish, every law-abiding cus-
> tom and if afterwards I should wish to deny and
> return to Jewish superstition, or shall be found eat-
> ing with the Jews or feasting with them or secretly
> conversing with them and condemning the Christian
> religion instead of openly confuting them and con-
> demning their vain faith, then let the trembling of

Cain, and the leprosy of Gehazi cleave to me, as well as the legal punishments to which I acknowledge myself liable, and may my soul be set down with Satan and the devils. Furthermore, I accept all customs, rites, legalisms and feasts of the Romans, sacrifices, prayers, purifications with water, santifications by Pontius Maximus, propitiations and feasts, the New Sabbath—the Sol Dei (Sun Day)—all new chants and observances, all foods and drinks of the Romans in the New Roman Religion."

If Christians have ever wondered why Yeshua and the apostles celebrated Passover, but the Church celebrates Easter, or why Yeshua and the apostles celebrated the Feast of Tabernacles and the Church celebrates Christmas, then you are very close to finding the answers. Was it Adonai's will for the "Jewish" customs and people to be thrown out of the Church? Was it Adonai's will for the Nazarenes to be thrown out of the synagogues? Was it Adonai's will for prayer to be the weapon that divided His people instead of uniting them?

It is interesting to note, however, that this benediction takes the twelfth spot, and perhaps even in its evil intent, the malediction serves a prophetic purpose. To the twelve tribes who were scattered among Jews and Christians with these two creeds, perhaps the negation of the benediction will someday mark their return to one faith. Is the Church ready to turn back to the Hebraic roots of their faith? Is the Jew ready to drop this malediction from the Shemoneh Esrei so that it will once again have the power of the Eighteen Benedictions instead of the nineteen this curse created?

CHAPTER NINETEEN

Tzaddikim
The Righteous

Upon the righteous, upon the devout, upon the elders of the remnant of Your people the family of Israel, on the remnant of their scholars in houses of study, on the righteous converts and on us may Your compassion be aroused, please Adonai our God, and give a good reward to all who truly believe in Your Name. Make us to walk with them, and may we never feel ashamed, for in You we trust, and we depend upon Your great compassion. Blessed are You, Adonai, Supporter and Assurance of the Righteous.

The scriptural basis for this benediction is "*and the righteous man is the foundation of the world.*"[98] This principle is renewed in the Book of James:

> But above all, my brethren, do not swear, either by heaven or by earth or with any other oath; but your yes is to be yes, and your no, no, so that you may not fall under judgment. Is anyone among you suffering? {Then} he must pray. Is anyone cheerful? He is to sing praises. Is anyone among you sick? {Then}

---

98. Proverbs 10:25.

he must call for the elders of the church and they
are to pray over him, anointing him with oil in the
name of the Lord; and the prayer offered in faith
will restore the one who is sick, and the Lord will
raise him up, and if he has committed sins, they will
be forgiven him. Therefore, confess your sins to one
another, and pray for one another so that you may
be healed. The effective prayer of a righteous man
can accomplish much.[99]

The word *fervent* in the passage denotes being zealous
with knowledge. In this same verse, the word *righteous* means
executing an act the correct way. "*The effectual fervent prayer
of a righteous man avails much.*" A righteous man's prayers
can avail more than the average prayer. James implies that a
righteous man not only has zeal in his prayer, but he has an
educated form of zeal. The most effective prayers are not only
heart-felt, but they are prayed according to Scripture, which
is God's will. The Shemonei Esrei is based upon Scripture,
and it is like quoting God's Word back to Him, which cannot
be contrary to His will unless our timing or motive is poor.

This prayer is unique because it contains all twenty-two
letters of the Hebrew alphabet, and it is the thirteenth blessing. This is designed to correspond to the Thirteen Attributes
of Mercy. It is also the gematria of two important words,
ahavah, or love, and *echad*, or unity. Unity is an important
part of this prayer because one prays to be included in the
congregation of the righteous.

The prayer for the devout and the righteous converts
includes those from the nations who have taken hold of the
prayer garment of The Jew. Cornelius is described as a devout
man. An example of righteous converts is found in Acts 2. The
men who hear the Word in Acts 2 are Jews and proselytes. Each
convert gathers in Jerusalem specifically to be obedient to the

---

99. James 5:12-16.

Torah, which commands males to appear three times a year in Jerusalem. Talmud Shabbos 146a says that all the righteous Gentiles of every generation who were destined to join the covenant were gathered at Mt. Sinai. If you are a righteous Gentile, you were there!

The Names of God in this benediction are *Mishan L'Tzaddik* and *Mivtach L'Tzaddik*, Supporter and Assurance of the Righteous. *Mishan* means that He fortifies us with power to endure adversity. *Mivtach* is assurance that He will answer prayer. *L'tzaddik* reminds the supplicant that the ultimate goal is to become a *tzaddik*, a righteous one growing in spiritual matters and intensified faith daily. The benediction also affirms Paul's exhortation to Timothy, "*Therefore I exhort first of all that supplications, prayers, intercessions, and giving of thanks be made for all men, for kings and all who are in authority, that we may lead a quiet and peaceable life in all godliness and reverence.*"[100]

---

100. I Timothy 2:1-2.

CHAPTER TWENTY

Binyan Yerushalayim
Rebuilding Jerusalem

And to Jerusalem, Your city, may You return with compassion,
and may You rest in it, as You have said. May You rebuild it
speedily in our days as an eternal building, and may you
speedily set up the throne of your servant David within it.
Blessed are You, Adonai, Builder of Jerusalem.

To those looking for Messiah, this prayer is reminiscent of Yeshua's words to Jerusalem: "You will not see Me again until you say, '*Baruch haba b'shem Adonai.*" As disciples of Yeshua, it is important to join the faithful who welcome Messiah Yeshua, "*Blessed is He who comes in the Name of the Lord.*"

King David wrote about the City of David, "*The built-up Jerusalem is like a city that is united together.*"[101] For David, Jerusalem served as a unifying social force for all the tribes of Israel, and all Israel converged on Jerusalem for the festivals of the Lord. One day the Son of David will likewise build up Jerusalem and make it a unifying force for all Israel, as the Prophets testify. David also sang, "*You will arise and have mercy on Zion, for the appointed time has come, for Your servants have*

---

101. Psalm 122:3.

desired her stones and cherished her dust.[102] Jerusalem is the place for all Israel to observe the appointed times, to desire her stones and to cherish her dust. What is more beautiful than the pink stones of Jerusalem at sunset? What is more cherished than the dust? The dust is a testimony of the covenant made with Abraham that has unfolded through the ages, culminating in the gospel of Yeshua, for Abraham's descendants are *"as numerous as the dust of the earth"*[103] through the blood of Messiah Yeshua.

When reciting this blessing for the rebuilding of Jerusalem, one may experience intense longing for the Holy Land and the Sacred City. Although we know that Adonai will not arise in compassion until the appointed time, yet we pray according to His Word that He will have mercy and rebuild not only physical Jerusalem, but draw down Jerusalem above. Jerusalem is a city that exists in two levels, in two worlds. Heavenly Jerusalem exists in complete harmony with God's will. This corresponds to part of the Disciples' Prayer, *"may thy will be done on earth as it is in heaven."* The earthly Jerusalem is to increase in knowledge and obedience of Adonai, and to model itself after the heavenly Jerusalem. Adonai rests in the heavenly Jerusalem, and He will soon rest in an earthly Jerusalem that is completely instructed and obedient to His will.

One of the main complaints of Judaism is that Yeshua, for all His wonderful teaching and miracles, never gathered the exiles or rebuilt Jerusalem as the City of David, free from the unclean influences.[104] To the doubters, Yeshua never found the exiles of Israel, never united them, never drove the unclean nations from Jerusalem, never restored the government of Israel in righteousness, and never sent the Torah

---

102. Psalm 102:14-15.

103. Genesis 13:16.

104. Aryeh Kaplan, *The Real Messiah*, (New York: National Conference of Synagogue Youth, 1976), 54.

from Jerusalem; in fact, it was destroyed and given completely into the hands of the Gentiles, and for decades, no Jew could enter Aelia Capitolina, the name given conquered Jerusalem by her Roman oppressors.

Yeshua, however, did these things, not in one lifetime, but He is doing it generation by generation. His people are less than perfect, and there is mistrust among those who are brothers in Messianic hope; nevertheless, the Word of God is reaching the farthest corners of the earth. Israel is being regathered to the Land through the agency of both Jew and righteous Gentile. The Torah is going forth from Jerusalem. Messiah will return and bring these things to complete fulfillment, perfecting, rebuilding, cleansing, and teaching righteousness. Psalm 147:2 says that the Builder of Jerusalem is gathering the outcasts of Israel. It is written in the present tense to note that it is an ongoing process. There have been generations in which no one could identify a tangible rebuilding of Israel, but in that generation events took place that affected a later one's ability to take larger strides. While Martin Luther was a confirmed anti-Semite, the reforms he set in motion made freedom from the Roman church possible. The regathering of Israel has been slower than watching a tree grow, yet it is in motion.

CHAPTER TWENTY-ONE

Malkhut Beit David
Kingdom of the House
of David

*May the offspring of Your servant David soon flourish, and
lift up his pride through Your salvation, for we hope for Your
Salvation all day long. Blessed are You, Adonai, Who makes
the pride of Salvation to flourish.*

This blessing is a continuation of the prayer for Jerusalem,
for the Son of David's return is necessary for the building
of Jerusalem. The Son of David is *"Tzmach David Avdekha."* In
English it is "The offspring of your servant, David…" *Tzmach* is
translated as offspring. It can mean a branch or shoot. The
Tzmach David, or the Righteous Branch, is known to be something that spreads very slowly, as slowly as a vine spreading. As
with the tree, its progress is measured over time. Almost two
thousand years after Yeshua rejoined His Father, He nevertheless flourishes all over the Earth like a vine. *"And there shall blos-
som forth a sprout from the stem of Jesse and a branch shall grow
out of his roots. And the spirit of Adonai shall rest upon Him."*[105]
Zechariah teaches that the Messiah's name will be Tzemach, literally the growth of the plant. Messianic redemption is not one
violent act of upheaval, but also a natural, progressive process.

---

105. Isaiah 11:1-2.

Yeshua's Vine has taken the Torah throughout the Earth; many are coming to faith in Him and His Words.

The letters of Hebrew words sometime may be spelled backward to produce opposite meanings. The opposite of Tzmach, the Righteous Branch, is *chametz*, the leaven cleaned from Israelite homes at Passover. The leavened pride of *chametz* contrasts with the "pride of salvation" in this prayer. Pride usually is touted as a bad thing, but as with all things God created, there are good and bad aspects to draw from. Psalm 132:17 says, "*There (in Jerusalem) I shall cause pride to flourish for David.*"

"Pride" in both the Psalm and the blessing is the Hebrew word *keren*. It can also mean "horn." Horns, like pride, have two aspects. One aspect of a horn is strength. A bull takes his horns and shakes them at all who threaten his herd, and with the horns he will push or gore the enemy. On the other hand, a horn is how the ancient oil of anointing is carried. The commentary on Jewish law, the Gemara, sheds light on the horn of salvation.

> The Gemara in its analysis of the alefbet (Shabbos 104a) says that the letter *cahf* stands for the crown that the Holy One, Blessed is He, will place on the heads of the righteous in the world to come. According to Kehilat Yaakov, the word that refers to the Crown is *keren (koof-reish-nun sofeet)*. This word signifies the horn of an animal, or a ray of light. We find it as a verb in the Torah's description of Moses when he descended from Mt. Sinai: '*The skin of his face radiated.*' A horn is like a crown because both radiate from the head. The English word crown is phonetically similar to *keren* (horn); both have the same three consonant sounds in the same order: K. R. N.[106]

---

106. Mattityahu Glazerson, *Torah, Light and Healing*, (Jerusalem: Lev Eliyahu Foundation, 1993), 165.

This prayer requests that the "pride" or "horn" be increased. Both the strength of salvation (Yeshua) and the anointing of salvation (Yeshua) will grow and increase, just as the Tzmach grows and increases. This prayer is not only the expectation of Messiah's return, it actually names Him, *Yeshua*. Though the spreading of the Vine is slow, this benediction petitions for the process to speed up. As goes the Vine, so go the branches, so believers pray to be blessed with increasing strength and anointing as the influence of the gospel and the commandments of Adonai spread throughout the earth. The Name of God used in this benediction is *Matzmiach Keren Yeshua*, The Lifter of Yeshua's Pride: Glory, Strength, and Anointing.

CHAPTER TWENTY-TWO

Kabbalat Tefillah
Acceptance of Prayer

Hear our voice, Adonai our God, have mercy and be compassionate to us, and accept our prayer with willingness and compassion, for you are God Who hears prayers and supplications. From before You, our King, turn us not away empty-handed. For You hear the prayer of Your people Israel with compassion. Blessed are You, Adonai, Who hears prayer.

The Kabbalat Tefillah reads, "Hear our voice," not hear "my" voice. It's a group prayer for the Commonwealth of Israel. The principle of Jewish prayer is to bring all Israel into unity, a principle frequently overlooked in mainstream Christianity. The number of Christian denominations is staggering, which can be positive in its diversity, but has wreaked havoc on its corporate identity. Judaism, although it has factions, almost universally accepts a corporate identity in this common prayer.

The Names of God are "Merciful Father" or "*Av Rachaman.*" What father can impassively refuse to respond to his infant's pleas? "*Out of the mouths of babes He has perfected praise.*"[107] A baby begs for food or relief, unable to

---

107. Matthew 21:16.

think that his father owes him anything, or that he deserves anything; the infant merely cries out as a result of hunger or discomfort. This prayer becomes perfect praise, and a model for us. Our heart cries may be unintelligible to others, just infant babbling, but the Father knows exactly what we need. Another Name of God in this benediction is *Shomea Tefillah*, the Hearer of Prayer.

CHAPTER TWENTY-THREE

Avodah
Temple Service

Be favorable, Adonai, our God, toward Your people Israel and their prayer, and restore the service to the Holy of Holies of Your Temple. Accept the fire-offerings of Israel and their prayer with love and favor, and may the service of Your people Israel always be favorable to You. May our eyes behold Your returning to Zion in compassion. Blessed are You, Adonai, the Restorer of His Presence to Zion.

There is a connection between the Disciples' Prayer and the Avodah. The Disciples' Prayer acknowledges, *Thine is the Kingdom, the power and the glory.* This is a quote from David's dedication of the Temple offerings he had collected for Solomon.[108] The dedication of the Temple is deeply rooted in thanksgiving and freewill offerings, and offerings of thanksgiving were an important part of the Temple service. Ancient prayer and offering went hand in hand. It is believed that these daily prayer offerings were accumulated during the week, and made up the substance of that which was later brought to the sanctuary during worship time. Money was frequently used as a thanksgiving offering to accompany

---

108. I Chronicles. *29:8*

prayers. Yeshua encouraged this practice, and sat unembarrassed to watch not only the gifts that people brought into the Temple, but the attitude of the giver. Paul teaches this practice of setting aside thank offerings during the work week.

> Now concerning the collection for the saints, as I
> have given orders to the churches of Galatia, so you
> must do also: On the first day of the week let each
> one of you lay something aside, storing up as he may
> prosper, that there be no collections when I come.
> And when I come, whomever you approve by your
> letters I will send to bear your gift to Jerusalem.[109]

This is not necessarily written Torah, but a *halakhic* ruling, or Jewish custom passed on to the Gentiles. The collections are not bound for the Temple, but for the maintenance of the apostles in Jerusalem who had committed all they owned to the spreading of the gospel. Paul taught that it is not improper for these thank offerings to be redirected to the congregation at Jerusalem to ensure their maintenance and the ongoing missionary work. This benediction reminds the supplicant that it is still proper to give thank offerings to those who serve the Body of Messiah, and points to a reality rapidly approaching that generation. The Temple was soon to be destroyed, and believers in Yeshua would be scattered. The Temple was making a transition from a physical stone building to physical human buildings. The appropriation of thank offerings to the Temple was being adjusted to meet the needs of the many new Temples of the Holy Spirit. This benediction is number seventeen, which corresponds to the numerical value of the word *tov*, or good. "*Hodu l'Adonai ki tov*," "Give thanks to the Lord, for He is good."

While it may not seem appropriate in our generation to offer a fire-offering, this blessing holds some deep truths

---

109. I Corinthians 16:1-3.

concerning the animal sacrifice. Lurking inside of every human heart is a wild beast, the evil inclination. When man surrenders himself to the animal impulse, he rejects the Divine gift which is to distinguish him from the beasts of the earth. Part of our offering has not changed since animal sacrifices were brought to the Temple, which is the sacrifice of a broken spirit and a contrite heart, the calves of our lips. This benediction is an offering of the wild beast inside as a fiery offering on Adonai's altar. It is equivalent to "crucifying the flesh."

To lay one's self upon the brazen altar of the Temple is to imitate Messiah Yeshua, who had no sin to burn up; nevertheless, He laid Himself there on our behalf. We are urged to bring forth works worthy of that sacrifice made for us. For us, however, the brazen altar will be a painful experience as it purges our souls, our animal appetites, and desires. As we learn the Torah, it is a fiery law, and it burns and purifies us. Our goal is to purge as much of our animal instinct on that altar in this physical body as we can, so that like Yeshua, what is there to burn at the judgment?

It is important to recognize the fire of the altar as the Word of God that purges us:

> Now this is the blessing with which Moses the man
> of God blessed the children of Israel before his
> death. And he said: "The Lord came from Sinai, And
> dawned on them from Seir; He shone forth from
> Mount Paran, And He came with ten thousands of
> saints; From His right hand came a **fiery law** for
> them. Yes, He loves the people; All His saints are in
> Your hand; They sit down at Your feet; Everyone
> receives Your words. Moses commanded a Torah for
> us, a heritage of the congregation of Jacob.[110]

---

110. Deuteronomy 33:1-4

One fleshly altar sacrifice is the eyesight, which this prayer consecrates. "May our eyes behold your returning to Zion in compassion." In the future when Messiah returns to Zion, He will reveal His glory to Israel, "*They shall see eye to eye when Adonai returns to Zion*."[111] The eye is a marvelous part of our bodies. As complicated as it is, even the tiniest speck of dust can interfere with vision and force a person to shut his eye tightly. This can also occur with spiritual vision. It takes only a small speck of dust to cause one to shut his eyes to Truth, so it is important to guard spiritual vision. Isaiah said, "*He who shuts his eyes from seeing evil...his eyes shall behold the King in all His beauty*."[112] Believers ask for the privilege of utilizing the eyes for holy matters, and to be spared from profaning them.

Our altar service is not all unpleasant, though. If we are faithful to crucify the flesh on the outer brazen altar, we may enter the Holy Place to offer incense on the golden altar. Our senses are then filled with delights of the Holy Place: fresh bread, sweet-smelling clouds of incense, the soft and intimate light of the menorah, the precious gold metals, and the elegant, colorful tapestries. Most of all, we are filled with the Presence of Adonai. The Name of God in this benediction is *HaMachzir Sh'khinato L'tzion*, or The Restorer of His Presence (*Shekhinah*) to Zion.

---

111. Isaiah 52:8.
112. Isaiah 33:15-17.

CHAPTER TWENTY-FOUR

Hodaat
Thanksgiving

We thank You, for it is You Who are Adonai, the God of our forefathers forever; the Rock of our lives, Shield of our Salvation (Yeshua!) are You from generation to generation. We will thank You and declare Your praise for our lives, which are in Your hands, our souls that are entrusted to You, Your daily miracles, and for Your wonders and favors at all times: evening, morning, and afternoon. The Good One, for Your compassions were not exhausted, and the Compassionate One, for Your kindnesses never ended; we have always put our hope in You. For all these, may Your Name be blessed and exalted, Our King, continually forever. Everything alive will thank You, selah! And praise Your Name in truth forever, for it is Good. O God of our salvation and help, selah. The Good God. Blessed are You, Adonai, Your Name is the Good One, and to You it is proper to give thanks.

It is appropriate that this is the eighteenth blessing of the Shemonei Esrei because *chai*, life, has a numerical value of eighteen, and the purpose of life is to recognize God's kindness and to thank Him for it by devoting one's life to His service, as the prophet says, "*the living, only the living will gratefully praise You.*[113] This blessing is composed of exactly eighty-six words, which is the numerical value of *Elohim*, the Name of the Creator, and also the same value as *hatbah*, or nature. This prayer blesses and thanks God for creating all the wonders of nature that man continually enjoys: "Everything alive will gratefully acknowledge You, selah." If one thanks Adonai for these unseen wonders daily, then he is reminded of the power of Elohim to maintain the creation through the power of His word, and he can never become callous to the miracles and wonders that sustain the universe. Names of God in this blessing are *Tsur Chayenu*, Rock of Our Lives, *Magen Yishenu*, Shield of Our Salvation, *HaTov*, The Good One, and *Hamrachem*, The Compassionate One.

This prayer begins in Hebrew with "*Modim anachnu lakh*," which has a numerical value of one hundred. It means "we gratefully thank You." In the second century, many Jews prayed one hundred short-sentence prayers throughout the day. In his letter to the Thessalonians, Paul refers to these prayers, which are actually blessings, when he says, "*Pray without ceasing.*"[114]

113. Isaiah 38:19.
114. I Thessalonians 5:17.

CHAPTER TWENTY-FIVE

Shalom
Peace

Establish peace, goodness, blessing, life, graciousness, kindness, and compassion upon us and upon all of Your people Israel. Bless us Our Father, all of us together, with the light of Your countenance, for with the light of Your countenance You gave us, Adonai our God, the Torah of life and a love of kindness, righteousness, blessing, compassion, life, and peace. And may it be good in Your eyes to bless us and to bless all of Your people Israel, in every season and in every hour with Your peace. Blessed are You, Adonai, Who blesses His people Israel with peace.

The serene person is in control of his thoughts and feelings; he is not at the mercy of external events that swing unpredictably and attempt to influence human temperaments and moods. Peace is the conclusion of the Amidah because prayer serves as a substitute for the Temple sacrifice, and at the conclusion of the sacrificial service, the priests blessed the Jewish people, ending with *"and may He grant you peace* "[115] Five other qualities besides peace in this blessing allude to the six blessings of the *Birkhat Kohanim,* the Priestly

---

115. Numbers 6:26.

Blessing: goodness, blessing, graciousness, kindness, and compassion. Together, these are the substance of the Birkhat Kohanim:

> May Adonai bless you and keep you
> May Adonai make His face shine upon you
> And be gracious to you
> May Adonai lift up His countenance upon you
> And give you peace

"With the light of your countenance" in the Shalom corresponds to the second part of the Priestly Blessing, "*May Adonai illuminate His countenance for you and be gracious to you.*" When God shines the light of His face, He imparts the ability to understand His ways and to recognize a personal mission in attaining His goals for the world. Another request is "The Torah of life and a love of kindness, righteousness, blessing, compassion, life, and peace." These seven blessings represent the seven flames of the Menorah of the Holy Temple, which radiated Divine light to the entire world.[116] As all are required to inquire about, or pray, for the peace of Jerusalem, the supplicant adds, "Who blesses His people Israel with peace." We pray with intense fervor that Adonai bring enduring peace to our beloved Land. When Messiah arrives, He will begin with a call for peace, as it says, "*How beautiful upon the mountains are the feet of him who brings good tidings, who announces peace.*"[117] The word *shalom* means peace in a way that is *shalem*, complete and wholesome.

---

116. Feurer, 267.
117. Isaiah 52:7.

CHAPTER TWENTY-SIX

Conclusion:
Personal Supplication

*My God, guard my tongue from evil and my lips from speaking
deceit. To those who curse me, let my soul be silent, and let my
soul be like dust to everyone. Open my heart to Your Torah, and
then my soul will seek Your commandments. As for all those
who plot evil against me, quickly nullify their counsel and disrupt their plans. May it be Your will, Adonai, my God and the
God of my forefathers, that human jealousy may not rise
against me, nor may I be jealous of others; may I not be angry
today, and may I not anger You. Rescue me from the Evil
Inclination, and place in my heart submissiveness and humility.
O our King and our God, cause Your Name to be unified in
Your world; rebuild Your city, lay the foundation of Your House,
perfect Your Sanctuary; gather in the scattered exiles, redeem
Your sheep, and make glad Your congregation. Act for Your
Name's sake; act for Your right hand's sake, act for Your Torah's
sake, act for Your sanctity's sake so that Your beloved ones may
be given rest; let Your right hand save and respond to me. May
the words of my mouth and the thoughts of my heart find
graceful favor before You, Adonai, my Rock and my Redeemer.*

*He Who makes peace in His high places, may He make peace
upon us, and upon all Israel. Amein.*

May it be Your will, Adonai our God and the God of our fore-fathers, that the holy Temple be rebuilt speedily in our days. Grant us our portion in Your Torah, and may we serve You there with reverence as in ancient days and years. Then the descendants of Judah and Jerusalem will be pleasing to Adonai as in days of old and in former years.

The final supplication of the Shemonei Esrei serves as a time for the petitioner to insert personal spontaneous prayers. Before the 120 men of the Great Assembly composed the standard text of the Amidah, prayer was spontaneous heart cries. The standard text of the Amidah was not designed to stifle those spontaneous prayers, but to inspire them. We are given many guidelines for prayer in Scripture, and there are hundred of books, curricula, and seminars that teach Christian patterns of prayer. Even Yeshua taught the disciples a pattern of prayer, which if closely examined, contains an abbreviated version of the Standing Prayer. Having a framework for our daily prayers is an aid to forgetful men, who may be so consumed with the troubles of the day that they forget important aspects of prayer, such as thanksgiving, forgiveness, service, and praise. If we have a framework for prayer that includes all the important components of Scriptural prayer, then we are even more confident in our approach with personal, spontaneous petitions and worship. Many of these petitions will remind us of issues we need to bring to our King and Father's attention. One may think of the Amidah as the business of the Kingdom we bring to the King that precedes the more intimate family matters we bring to our Comforter and Father.

The first request of personal supplication is for the petitioner's lips to be guarded from evil and deceit. These words paraphrase King David's advice to avoid gossip and slander: *"Guard your tongue from evil, and your lips from speaking deceitfully."*[118] In the Apostolic Scriptures, this necessity is renewed:

---

118. Psalm 34:14

He who would love life and see good days, Let him
refrain his tongue from evil, And his lips from
speaking deceit. Let him turn away from evil and do
good; Let him seek peace and pursue it. For the eyes
of the Lord are on the righteous, And His ears are
open to their prayers; But the face of the Lord is
against those who do evil."[119]

In the preceding verses, Peter and King David say that
this is the formula for the person who desires life. It is appropriate that just as the Shemoneh Esrei opens with a desire for
Adonai to open the lips to praise Him, so it closes with a
prayer to keep the lips closed to evil. The Apostle James wrote
much about the evil that the wicked tongue causes not only
to those around him, but to the actual Creation itself.

In the Midrash, a collection of ancient Jewish illustrative
teachings, a story is told of Rabbi Shimon ben Gamliel. The
rabbi sent his servant, Tavi, to buy some "good food." Tavi was
a wise servant, and he purchased a tongue for Rabbi Gamliel.
Rabbi Gamliel sent Tavi again to buy some food, but this time
he asked for "bad food." Again, Tavi returned with a tongue!
The rabbi asked his wise servant to explain how a tongue
could be both good food and bad food. Tavi replied to Rabbi
Gamliel: "When a tongue speaks good, there is nothing better,
but when it doesn't speak good, there is nothing worse."

The enormous power of the tongue has impact in heaven.
Man was created to be the spokesman of the universe. He is
the only creature selected by God to be a "speaking spirit." As
such, he defines and judges the world around him and speaks
those judgments into the spiritual realms. In other words,
what the Father in Heaven hears about His Creation, your
family, your friends, your coworkers, your nation, even the
driver on the street, is what you testify concerning them. If
you speak more negative things than positive about the world

around you, it's the spoken testimony that Heaven hears, and ultimately the spoken testimony you give will justify or condemn you. The Hebrew word for "tongue" is *lashon*, a word that also refers to the balancing bar at the top of the balancing scale; it is the part of the mechanism that tilts the scales. It is the tongue that also weighs all man's actions, and it tips the balance in the direction of innocence or guilt. The scales of justice are under the jurisdiction of the tongue, for as the Proverb says: "*Death and life are in the hands of the tongue, and whoever loves either will eat of its fruit.*"[120]

You as a human being absolutely control the earthly testimony spoken about your world, although you do not control the judgments made. When your earthly judgment on the world, or even God's People, contradicts the heavenly decrees, you will find yourself under judgment, as did Balaam, whose will to curse Israel contradicted the Heavenly decree to bless it. Although the Holy Spirit influenced Balaam to bless Israel, he later contrived a wicked plan to place a stumblingblock before her, and he met his demise. It is critical to guard the tongue from speaking anything that we know is contrary to Adonai's will for us and His Creation, which is ours to uphold with the power of His Word.

The benediction requests the inner strength to respond, "*to those who curse me, let my soul be silent.*" One of the great benefits of sincere prayer is that it suffuses the supplicant with a sense of complete calm and equanimity. It makes no difference to the humble, well-balanced person whether he is praised or insulted by others. His self-esteem comes from within himself. The word *simchah*, joy, contains the root *machah*, to erase. If one truly wishes to rejoice, he must first erase his conscious desire to place his feelings above others'. He must erase himself.

Another passage of the closing supplication is, "Act for your name's sake..." This section of requests sums up the

---

120. Proverbs 18:21

essential purpose of all our prayers. Israel's main concern is not for personal welfare, but to intensify God's sanctity and glory in the world. Thus, at the end of the Amidah, all Israel beseeches Adonai to end the exile for the sake of His Name and sanctity. "For My own sake, for My own sake, I will do it…"[121] is a reference to the coming Messiah.

A significant passage is "Grant us our share in your Torah." To the Jews are given the "*oracles of God*,"[122] the Torah and Prophets, which they've zealously protected and preserved for the world. For eighteen hundred years, though, Gentile believers have failed to take hold of their full heritage in the Torah, their portion and inheritance obtained through Yeshua's blood. According to Paul, their portion in the Torah is "good, just, holy"[123] and "spiritual." A denomination means "little nation." So many denominations are defined by how much of the Torah they accept as much as how they choose to live it. Some who purport that they are not "under the law" observe the Levitical commandments for tithing and prohibiting incest, yet accuse others who choose more commandments as legalists. How much Torah makes one a legalist? Isn't it time that we no longer define ourselves by the set of commandments we choose, quit forming little nations, and acknowledge that we are all part of the Commonwealth of Israel, the truly One Nation Under God? Just as Israel is Adonai's inheritance and portion, so He has given the strong sons and daughters of Israel all His Word for our portion and inheritance.

Some verses of Scripture make statements that encompass the whole of Scripture. One example is the Shema, "*Hear O Israel, the Lord your God is One*," coupled with "*You shall love your neighbor as yourself.*"[124] Another example is in

---

121. Isaiah 48:11.
122. Romans 3:2.
123. Romans 7:12-14.
124. Matthew 22:37-38

Habakkuk, *"The just shall live by faith."*[125] The closing supplication of the Shemoneh Esrei prays for the ability to worship from Jerusalem "with reverence, as in ancient days and years." This request is based on Deuteronomy 10:12, which asks Israel the sum of all commandments, *"And now Israel, what does Adonai your God ask of you? Only that you fear Adonai your God."*

This final petition for Temple restoration corresponds to Solomon's Temple dedication prayer, that wherever Adonai's people are dispersed, that they would remember their share in the Torah and turn toward the Temple to pray. For the Jew first, Solomon prays:

> When they sin against You, and You become angry
> with them and deliver them to the enemy, and they
> take them captive to a land far or near; yet when
> they come to themselves in the land where they were
> carried captive, and repent, and make supplication
> to You in the land of their captivity, saying, 'We have
> sinned, we have done wrong, and have committed
> wickedness'; and when they return to You with all
> their heart and with all their soul in the land of
> their captivity, and pray toward their land which
> You gave to their fathers, the city which You have
> chosen, and toward the temple which I have built
> for Your name: then hear from heaven Your dwelling
> place their prayer and their supplications, and main-
> tain their cause.

For the Righteous Gentiles, who have gained admittance through Messiah Yeshua's blood, Solomon prays:

> Moreover, concerning a foreigner, who is not of Your
> people Israel, but who comes from a far country for

---

125. Habbukuk 2:4.

the sake of Your great name and Your mighty hand and Your outstretched arm, when they come and pray in this temple; then hear from heaven Your dwelling place, and do according to all for which the foreigner calls to You, that all peoples of the earth may know Your Name and fear You, as do Your people Israel, and that they may know that this temple which I have built is called by Your Name.[126]

Let the Commonwealth of Israel turn toward Jerusalem and pray, "My Lord, open my lips that my mouth may declare Your praise."

---

126. 2 Chronicles 6:32-33

CHAPTER TWENTY-SEVEN

Additional Prayer:
The Vidui Confession
Putting Your House in Order
According to Cornelius' Prayer

After the Minchah prayers, Jews often follow up with an additional prayer called the Vidui, or Confessional prayer. The reason for this is obvious, for repentance is an important aspect of our relationship with Adonai. There are mysteries of the Kingdom, however, concerning the principle of confessing sin. These mysteries are hidden to those who have never had the opportunity to study the Biblical Hebrew text. Unto His *talmidim*, however, Yeshua has given to know the mysteries of the Kingdom. Many of the most profound statements of the Bible are concealed within the text of Leviticus, the Book of Purities. After all, it is from Leviticus that we first hear, "*Love your neighbor as yourself*," "*you shall be holy for I am holy*," and "*the life is in the blood*."

In verse 3 of Leviticus 16 is the priestly procedural plan for Yom Kippur. Yom Kippur is the Day of Atonement, and it is the holiest day of the Biblical calendar marked by prayer, fasting, and sacrifice. The Hebrew word *kapparah* denotes a covering, and thus an atonement. Verse 3 reads, "*With this shall Aaron come into the Sanctuary…*" It goes on to list a sin-offering, an *olah* (whole burnt) offering, and two he-goats. The high priest is to bring these while dressed in a plain linen tunic and breeches, sash, and turban, and he is to wash in water.

In Hebrew, the phrase reads, *"B'zot yavo Aharon el hakodesh..."* The Hebrew word that begins this procedure, *"b'zot"* is a compound word. It means "with this." The numerical value of b'zot is 408. This is also the sum value of three important symbolic words of Yom Kippur: *mammon* (money), *tzome* (fast), and *kol* (voice). This is an important hint to anyone who wishes to understand Yom Kippur. "With this" we come into the Sanctuary on Yom Kippur. The money, fasting, and voice are the practical applications of repentance, prayer, and charity, which are three main components of Yom Kippur. Indeed, the Prophet Isaiah affirms these three components of Yom Kippur: *"Is this not the fast that I have chosen: To loose the bonds of wickedness, To undo the heavy burdens, To let the oppressed go free, And that you break every yoke? Is it not to share your bread with the hungry, And that you bring to your house the poor who are cast out; When you see the naked, that you cover him, And not hide yourself from your own flesh?"*[127]

Cornelius is keeping and performing the very fast commanded on Yom Kippur by the Prophet Isaiah, and the tenth and eleventh chapters of Acts explain how:

> Acts 10:1-7 Now there was a man at Caesarea named Cornelius, a **centurion** of what was called the Italian cohort, a **devout** man and one who feared God with **all his household**, and **gave many alms to the Jewish people** and **prayed to God continually.** About the **ninth hour** of the day he clearly saw in a vision an angel of God who had just come in and said to him, "Cornelius!" And fixing his gaze on him and being much alarmed, he said, "What is it, Lord?" And he said to him, "**Your prayers and alms have ascended as a memorial before God.** "Now dispatch some men to Joppa and send for a man named Simon, who is also called Peter (Kefa); he is staying with a tanner named

---

127. Isaiah 58:6

Simon, whose house is by the sea." When the angel who was speaking to him had left, he summoned two of his servants and a devout soldier of those who were his personal attendants, and after he had explained everything to them, he sent them to Joppa.

Acts 11: Now the apostles and the brethren who were throughout Judea heard that the Gentiles also had received the word of God. And when Peter came up to Jerusalem, those who were circumcised took issue with him, saying, "You went to uncircumcised men and ate with them." But Peter began speaking and proceeded to explain to them **in orderly sequence,** saying, "I was in the city of Joppa praying; and in a trance I saw a vision, an object coming down like a **great sheet lowered by four corners** from the sky; and it came right down to me, and when I had fixed my gaze on it and was observing it I saw the **four-footed animals** of the earth and the wild beasts and the crawling creatures and the birds of the air. "I also heard a voice saying to me, 'Get up, Peter; kill and eat.' "But I said, 'By no means, Lord, for nothing **unholy or unclean** has ever entered my mouth.' "But a **voice from heaven answered a second time,**

'What God has **cleansed,** no longer consider **unholy.'** "This happened **three times,** and everything was drawn back up into the sky. "And behold, at that moment **three men** appeared at the house in which we were staying, having been sent to me from Caesarea. "The Spirit told me to go with them without misgivings.

These **six** brethren also went with me and we entered the man's **house.** "And he reported to us how he had seen the angel standing in his **house,** and saying, 'Send to Joppa and have Simon, who is

also **called Peter**, brought here; and he will **speak
words to you by which you will be saved**, you and
all your **household**.'

"And as I began to speak, the Holy Spirit fell upon
them just as He did upon us at the beginning. "And
I remembered the word of the Lord, how He used to
say, 'John **baptized with water**, but you will be **baptized with the Holy Spirit**.' "Therefore if God gave
to them the **same gift** as He gave to us also after
believing in the Lord Jesus Christ, who was I that I
could stand in God's way?" When they heard this,
they **quieted down** (shalom) and **glorified God**, saying,

"Well then, God has granted to the Gentiles also the
repentance that leads to life."

Solomon's inaugural Temple prayer requested for the
Gentiles, "*that all peoples of the earth may know Your name
and fear You, as do Your people Israel, and that they may know
that this temple which I have built is called by Your Name*."
Cornelius' attitude recorded in chapter 10 reflects exactly
this: *a devout man and one who feared God with all his household, and gave many alms to the Jewish people and prayed to
God continually*. Did Cornelius know the content of King
Solomon's prayer for him and his family? Did he know that
his prayers, fear of Heaven, desire for a House built by the
Holy One of Israel, and his kind deeds to the Jews would blow
open the door to repentance and life for all nations?

Acts 10 and 11 are pregnant with Hebrew insight according to the Hebrew letters and numbers:

- **6** brethren went with Peter/Kefa. Six is the letter *vav*,
  meaning a connection, the number of a man with head
  bowed.

- 4-footed animals in 4-cornered garment. Four is the letter *dalet*, the open door of repentance that leads to life, the four corners of the earth which would one day come to Elohim's radiance or glory.
- The garment was lowered 3 times and Cornelius sent 3 messengers. Three is the letter *gimel*, which is the rich man running to give gifts to the poor man. Kefa says in verse 17 that God gave to the Gentiles *"the same gift"* as the believing Jew.
- 2 times Kefa was commanded to "eat." Two is the letter *beit*, which is the House and the Temple
- 3 times the garment was lowered while the voice spoke 2 times in the vision = 5 Five is the letter *heh*, the number of femininity and the open channel to repentance for the sinner, the mercy of God.
- 9th hour, or **3:00 p.m.** to us, is the number of 9 months of pregnancy come to term, the promise to Abraham realized in Isaac
- centurion/100 = Genesis 17:17 Then Abraham fell on his face and laughed, and said in his heart, "Will a child be born to a man one hundred years old? And will Sarah, who is ninety years old, bear {a child?}" Genesis 21:5—Now Abraham was one hundred years old when his son Isaac was born to him. Abraham was the father of the nations, in him was the ability and the promise to bless ALL the nations of the world. Abraham was the father of all who first believed without the benefit of the covenant of circumcision. The non-Jew Cornelius, a centurion, has just been hewn from the rock Abraham and quarried from his mother Sarah. The pregnancy of the prophecy made to Abraham has just come to term and produced a healthy child!

There is another prophetic reference to the number 100 in Genesis 33:17-20:

Ya`akov journeyed to **Sukkot, built himself a house,**
and made **shelters for his cattle.** Therefore the name
of the place is called Sukkot. Ya`akov came in
shalom to the city of Shekhem, which is in the land
of Kana`an, when he came from Paddan-Aram; and
encamped before the city. He bought the parcel of
ground, where he had spread his tent, at the hand of
the children of Hamor, Shekhem's father, for **one
hundred pieces of money.** He **erected an altar** there,
and called it El-Elohe-Yisra'el.

Jacob in this context had just been transformed from
Jacob to Israel. He builds a House at Sukkot. The passage says
he came in shalom, just as the elders in Acts held their shalom
when Kefa revealed Adonai's purpose for the Gentiles.
Sukkot, or the Feast of Tabernacles, is the Feast of the
Nations, when all nations will come to worship King Yeshua:
Zechariah 14:16 "*And it shall come to pass that everyone who
is left of all the nations which came against Jerusalem shall go
up from year to year to worship the King, the Lord of hosts, and
to keep the Feast of Tabernacles.*"

Symbolically, Jacob pays the **100 pieces of earnest money
toward the repentance of the nations.** Cornelius, the ruler of
100, also gives money for the restoration of the nations by
giving to the Jews who have guarded the covenant for the
nations. Cornelius symbolically worships at the altar set so
many hundreds of years before by our father Jacob. You see,
the passage says that Jacob built shelters for his cattle. What
Kefa saw were **unclean** animals, but in Jacob's prophecy of
Sukkot, the shelters were for the **clean** four-footed animals,
the cattle. After all, doesn't the Psalmist say that Adonai owns
the cattle on the thousand hills?[128]

Acts 11 states that Kefa told his experience "*in orderly
sequence.*" He had just witnessed what it meant for the
Gentiles to put their houses in order. Cornelius was the first
one from the nations to experience Yom Kippur outside the

---

128. Psalm 50:10

physical precincts of the Temple. He followed Torah procedures of Yom Kippur, *"with this, with these things enter my holy Sanctuary."* He brought the sin offering, the verbal confession of the Shemoneh Esrei; he brought the good deeds of a heart tender toward God; he brought the money, the alms given to the Jews of his city. He brought the *olah* offering, the **whole** burnt offering, which was his whole family. These are the sacrifices of Yom Kippur which the non-Jew Cornelius brought, even outside the precincts of the physical Temple. Indeed, as the prayer is a *zikaron* to Adonai, we are reminded that *'On your days of rejoicing and your holy days and on your month's beginning, you shall blow the trumpets over your offerings that they may be to you memorial (zikaron) before your God."* The holy day trumpets heralded the *zikaron* offering of Cornelius' Yom Kippur heart condition, a Day of Atonement for the nations willing to repent and return to the Holy One of Israel.

Cornelius' prayer was a *zikaron* offering, a remembrance. This is a hint to his healing, his status change from unclean to clean. An unclean contamination in Hebrew is a *zav* זב. In the verse, *"Remember your Creator in the days of your youth, while the evil days come not..."* from Ecclesiastes, it reads in Hebrew, *"Zakhor Borehkha...,"* The first two letters spell *zav*, *zayin-veit* זב. The same Hebrew letter *beit* can be pronounced either *beit* or *veit*. In other words, if we find ourselves in a state of contamination in the flesh, the cure is to remember God before the really evil days come. We bring a *zikaron* offering of good deeds and sacrifices to Him. When these sacrifices and offerings are brought out of true repentance, then they become that *zikaron*, remembrance, and He dispatches His messengers with His Word to heal us.

According to the rabbinical commentary in the Talmud Berachot 22a, the words of the Torah are not susceptible to contamination. Torah is like fire (Jeremiah 23:29), which is also unaffected by uncleanness. Fire and words of Torah remain pure for all eternity. The Words that Kefa preached to Cornelius' house were pure fire for all eternity. It did the Jewish brethren no harm to be in the house of one considered unclean, for as when the woman with the issue of blood touched Yeshua, He, as the Pure Torah Fire of Eternity, could not be rendered unclean.

Adonai took away Cornelius' filthy clothes symbolized by the unclean things, and clothed him with priestly sacred vestments, fine linen of the four-cornered seamless garment like a sheet, which is in Hebrew a *kanfot,* a tunic, to which the fringes with the cord of blue are attached to remind an Israelite to *"keep the commandments to do them."* The *tallit,* the Jewish prayer garment, contains these ritual fringes as well. Adonai covered Cornelius' head with a turban, which was symbolized by Peter, Kefa, whose Hebrew name denotes the palm of the hand and kippa, or headcovering, as well as the atonement, Yom **Kippur,** the day of covering. The palm of the hand connoted by Kefa's name alludes to the Levitical ceremony of cleansing in which the high priest placed the oil into the palm of his right hand to anoint the unclean man who wished to return to the camp of Israel. Yeshua was the Fire on the altar that purified the Gentiles. The Father washed the Gentiles with water from the bronze laver of the Holy Spirit. The water in the laver represents moving to a deeper level of holiness as well.

Whether you are Jewish or not Jewish, do you want a personal Yom Kippur? Then do the works of Cornelius, your predecessor. Cornelius is described as a "devout" man. What other men of the Newer Testament are described as devout? Old Simeon was one devout man who was one of the first to testify of the infant Messiah Yeshua. He says, *"My eyes have seen your Salvation (Yeshua)."*[129] Another devout man is Ananias, *"Then a certain Ananias, a **devout** man according to the law (Torah), having a good testimony with all the Jews who dwelt there..."*[130] This is the disciple who welcomed Paul into the fellowship of those faithful to Messiah Yeshua. What about devout Gentiles who turned to Messiah Yeshua? Acts 13:43 *"Now when the congregation had broken up, many of the Jews and **devout proselytes** followed Paul and Barnabas, who, speaking to them, persuaded them to continue in the grace of God."* Notice that Paul encourages the proselyte Gentiles to

---

129. Luke 2:30.
130. Acts 22:12.

continue in God's grace. A proselyte is a Gentile who has joined himself to the Jewish people and the Torah community. Their faithfulness to the Torah is not discouraged, rather their continuation of walking in the Torah is called "the grace of God." To follow Cornelius' footsteps will require a rethinking of Paul's letters and our perception of God's grace.

Even Jews understand the commandments of Torah as grace to all nations. Quoting Rabbi Yirmiyahu, we have this astounding statement:

> "Whence do we know that a gentile who follows the Torah is to be regarded as equal to the High Priest? The Torah states: "Which if a man do, he shall live in them." Similarly, it is stated "open the gates that"—not the priests, Levites, and Israelites, but— "the righteous nation that keeps faithfulness may enter" (Isaiah 26:2)...

> Therefore, even a gentile who keeps Torah is regarded as equal to the High Priest."[131]

If the sons and daughters of Abraham desire to be loosed with the power of the first century apostles and congregations, they must shed eighteen hundred years of teaching that the Torah is bondage. There are sources that address Paul's comments to the Gentiles concerning the Law in balance with his deeds and the other authors of the New Testament, including Yeshua's own words: *"Do not think that I came to destroy the Law or the Prophets. I did not come to destroy but to fulfill. For assuredly, I say to you, till heaven and earth pass away, one jot or one tittle will by no means pass from the law (Torah) till all is fulfilled. Whoever therefore breaks one of the least of these commandments, and teaches men so, shall be called least in the kingdom of heaven; but whoever does and teaches them, he shall be called great in the kingdom of heaven."*[132]

---

131. Nechama Leibowitz. *New Studies in Vayikra*. Vol. 1. R. Fisch and A. Tomaschoff, Trans. (Israel: Haomanim Press, 1996), 258.

132. Matthew 5:17-20.

Paul's approach to the Torah is that it is good, pure, just, holy, able to reprove, rebuke, and to train in righteousness, but by no means to bring salvation. Living the Torah is the result of salvation, the fulfillment of the New Covenant. Bring good deeds, your money, your family, your whole house, your personal Temple of this body; fast, pray, and lift your voice in confession. Acknowledge as Lord the Restorer of the Earth, Messiah Yeshua, who came to repair the creation and to give the former glory to the Father. Learn to pray the prayer of Cornelius, the Shemoneh Esrei.

Find out what real confession of sin is. The Hebrew word *vadah* ודה is to confess. The confession is an integral part of not only the Shemoneh Esrei itself, but it is followed immediately at the Minchah, 3:00 P.M. prayers by something called the *vidui*, the confessional prayer. Possibly Cornelius has reached this portion of his Minchah prayers when the angel appears. Confession must come as a result of real pain and anguish over our shortfalls, our uncleanness, and our unfaithfulness. This is called *davah* דוה, which is grief or pain. Here are a few summary passages of the *vidui*:

> We are guilty: we betrayed, we robbed, we spoke slander. We caused perversion, we caused wickedness, we willfully sinned, we were violent, we falsely accused, we counseled evil, we were unfaithful, we scorned, we rebelled, we provoked, we turned away, we were perverse, we were careless, we persecuted, we were obstinate, we have corrupted, we were abominable, we have strayed and led others astray. We have turned away from Your commandments and from Your good judgment, and it has profited us nothing.

This is real repentance, to feel the pain of our sin and to offer everything at the altar, stripping ourselves of any personal glory that may have set itself above the Kingdom of Heaven. When this happens, the believing Jews of Acts "*glorified God*." Glory in Hebrew is *hod*, הוד. Mankind's first mission with the Creation was to glorify God, to bring His glory, radiance, and splendor, His *hod*, into the world in the proper order or sequence *heh-vav-dalet* הוד The glory that Adam had was a reflection of Elohim's *hod*. The glory of the Second Adam is the fullness of that glory.

Hebrew is read from right to left. Here are the Hebrew letters and meanings of *hod*, or **GLORY** הוד

heh, feminine, repentance, mercy = ה

vav, a man with bowed head, connection = ו

dalet, door open to the poor = ד

When the creation fell, the glory letters הוד were scrambled, and the end letter became the beginning letter, and the beginning letter the end letter, *dalet-vav-heh* דוה. This is the Hebrew word *davah*, which is pain, grief, and mourning. When the Creation was infected with sin, it tumbled into a realm of *davah*, grief, pain, mourning, and suffering. Sin distorts human lives and the life of all Creation. The *dalet*, whose value is 4, took precedence over the *heh*. The first letter became last, and the last letter became first. The unclean things represented by four-footed animals dominated, and Adam now had difficulty subduing the creation. Something called idolatry resulted, which is the worship of man with godlike attributes, fallen beasts, flying creatures, and creeping things. The great Rabbi Shaul teaches: Romans 1:22 *Professing to be wise, they became fools, and exchanged the **glory** of the incorruptible God for an image in the form of corruptible man and of birds and **four-footed animals** and crawling creatures. Therefore God gave them over in the lusts of their hearts **to impurity (uncleanness)**, so that their bodies would be dishonored among them. For they exchanged the truth of God for a lie, and worshiped and **served the creature rather than the Creator**, who is blessed forever. Amen."* In the realm of *davah*, man worships himself in his corruptible, impure form and the corrupted Creation, not understanding that what he values exists in fallen realm; fallen man cannot see the original glory of Adam until the Second Adam repairs his soul.

A process of creation repair was needed to restore correct order in the house so that the last could again become first and restore the Creation glory, the *hod*. All the nations needed repair so that they would serve the Creator rather than the created. *And He did so to make known the riches of His **glory** upon vessels of mercy, which He **prepared beforehand for glory**, even us, whom He also called, **not from among Jews only, but also from among Gentiles**.*[133] From the beginning, The Creator of the Universe planned to restore the glory to His Creation and mankind. His plan has been revealed to mankind progressively over the ages and marked in the pages of Scripture.

It is plain that Israel's part of the plan was to eventually bless all the nations of the world who looked for the first glory in the person of the Messiah Yeshua. The nations, who existed in the realm of *davah*, pain, grief, and suffering, and all Creation mourned and longed for the Restorer of all things, as Shaul teaches in Romans 8:21: *"that the creation itself also will be set free from its slavery to corruption into the freedom of the glory of the children of God."* Cornelius' prayer is ironic, for the Jews were the military and political slaves of the Romans, yet Kefa preaches the Restoration of all things to a Roman, and it is the Roman who is granted freedom from the corruption of *davah* and released back into the realm of glory.

Messiah Yeshua bore our *davah*, our pain and suffering, so that we could be made clean and have incorruptible bodies by inheriting the power of repentance and resurrection in our lives. Just as the Creation was spoken into perfection by the power of Elohim's speech, so we must confess-*vadah* ודה with our mouths that Yeshua the Messiah is Lord over us; we must speak His perfection aloud. *"For all have sinned and fallen short, from the glory of God.*[134]

What must occur for this house of glory to be set in order is repentance. The Vidui states: "Oh God, You are slow to anger,

---

133. Romans 9:23
134. Romans 3:23.

You are called the Lord of Mercy, and You have taught us the path of repentance." When Christians and Jews repent and confess, **vadah**, וָדָה , we begin the repair of the glory, and we, the *vav* ו or man, with head bowed, take the initiative with the first step of repentance. The *dalet* ד becomes the second letter, which is the redemptive open door of repentance bearing the blood of the Lamb on its doorpost, and is followed by the *heh* ה, which is the welcoming open channel of grace to restoration, the feminine aspect of God, His mercy. The restoration is the correction of the order, putting one's house, or personal Temple, in order. The proper order results in the glory of the Creator, which is then reflected in the created man.

The Apostle Paul taught that the woman is the glory of a man. This is the pattern of our restoration. As the woman reflects the glory of her husband, so men reflect the glory of the Most High. When the male and female are united, it results in praise, a restoration of the glory of God that existed in the beginning.

In like manner, Adonai's first glory or *hod* reflects on us, the man, the *vav*, second in order and submitted to the Holy Spirit. The final letter, the *dalet*, is the open door to the Kingdom of His Glory, his *hod*: heh, vav, dalet הוד. This is the Word of Elohim extending to the **four corners of the Earth**, the Kingdom of Messiah Yeshua. Once the process of Creation restoration is put in proper order, the Word of Adonai will go forth from Jerusalem to the four corners of the Earth, fulfilling the mystery of the Gentiles explained in Ephesians 2. All nations and creatures will be restored to their first covenant status through the power of the Word. This is what we call putting our lives in order, putting our houses in order, and putting this Temple of our bodies in order. When we do that, expect the Jews to cry, "Glory to God!" This is a mystery, as Shaul says in Ephesians 1:27, "*to whom God willed to make known what is the riches of the glory of this mystery among the Gentiles, which is Christ in you, the hope of glory*." And the writer of the letter to the Hebrews reminds the Jewish people of this principle as well: Hebrews 1:3 *"And He is the **radiance of His glory and the exact representation of His nature, and upholds all things by the word of His power.** When He had made **purification of sins,** He sat down at the right hand of the Majesty on high."*

This is the mystery of the Gentiles for which the Jews in Acts gave glory to the Most High. The ancient promises of restoration to the Creation, Abraham's blessing of all nations, and the House of Prayer for all nations had come to term, and new creations were being born in the Spirit of the Holy One of Israel. The Restorer of Israel had come and wrought such a work of Divine genius that no man could have conceived it. In the Vidui, we pray, "Help us, Oh God of our Salvation (Yeshua!), for the sake of Your Name's glory, rescue us and atone for our sins." The answer to the Vidui prayer has come to Jew and Gentile. His Name is Yeshua.

Messiah Yeshua is the key to the restoration and repair of the Creation, beginning with you and me. He has made purification of sins, and the process of purification is available to you through His power. You can reenter the Camp of Israel through the power of His holy life and be washed and anointed like a newborn. When we live in an attitude of repentance, prayer, and good deeds, we have a Yom Kippur experience every day of our lives, and we are part of the process of restoring the radiance of glory to the universe. To man, woman, or child, the Kingdom of Heaven is housework. Let us pray and work together with Messiah Yeshua to restore that glorious shine. If you would stand with Israel, then stand as Israel, and take hold of the Jewish prayer garment. Come with us.

Sources Cited

Bartleman, James. *What Really Happened at Azusa Street?* Northridge, CA: Voice Christian Publications, Inc., 04/08/20, 1962.

Berkowitz, Ariel and D'vorah. *Torah Rediscovered*. Littleton, CO: First Fruits of Zion, Inc., 04/08/20, 1996.

Chaim, Chofetz. *The Chofetz Chaim on Awaiting Messiah*. Southfield, MI: Targum Press, Inc., 04/08/20, 1993.

Cohen, Abraham. *Everyman's Talmud*. New York: Schocken, 04/08/20, 1949.

The Complete Artscroll Siddur. Translated by Nosson Scherman. New York: Mesorah Publications, Ltd., 04/08/20, 1995.

Edersheim, Alfred. *The Temple: Its Ministry and Services*. Peabody, MA: Hendrickson Publishers, 04/08/20, 1994.

Feuer, Avrohom Chaim. *Shemoneh Esrei*. New York: Mesorah Publications, Ltd., 1990.

The Five Books of Moses. Translated by Everett Fox. New York: Schocken, 04/08/20, 1995.

Glazerson, Mattityahu. *Torah, Light, and Healing*. Jerusalem: Lev Eliyahu Foundation, 04/08/20, 1993.

Gruber, Dan. *The Church and the Jews*. Hagerstown, MD: Serenity Books, 04/08/20, 1997.

Helevy, Hayim. *To Be a Jew*. USA: Basic Books, 04/08/20, 1972.

Horowitz, George. *The Spirit of Jewish Law: A Brief Account of Biblical and Rabbinical Jurisprudence*. New York: Bloch Publishing, 04/08/20, 1993.

Kaplan, Aryeh. *The Real Messiah*. New York: National Conference of Synagogue Youth, 1976.

Lamsa, George M. *Idioms in the Bible Explained and A Key to the Original Gospel*. San Francisco: HarperSanFranciscso, 04/08/20, 1985.

Leibowitz, Nechama. *New Studies in Vayikra*. Translated by R Fisch, and Tomaschoff. Volume I. Israel: Haomanim Press, 1996.

Munk, Elie. *The Call of the Torah.* Translated by E.S. Mazer. Shemot. New York: Mesorah Publications, Ltd., 04/08/20, 1994.

———. *The World of Prayer.* Translated by Henry Biberfield and Leonard Oschry. New York: P. Feldheim, 1954.

Munk, Michael. *The Wisdom in the Hebrew Alphabet.* New York: Mesorah Publications, Ltd., 04/08/20, 1983.

The Orthodox Jewish Brit Chadasha. Translated by Dr. Phillip E. Goble. 2d ed. New York: AFI International Publishers, 04/08/20, 1996.

Potok, Chaim. *The Chosen.* Robbie Benson. Twentieth Century Fox, 04/08/20, 1982.

Thomas, Amanda. "Between Passover and Easter." *Jerusalem Post* (Jerusalem), 26 April 2002, International, Pilgrim's Progress.

Zohar: The Book of Splendor. Edited by Gershom Scholem. New York: Schocken, 04/08/20, 1963.

AN ENGLISH TRANSLATION OF THE SHEMONEH ESREI

My Lord, open my lips that my mouth may declare Your Praise.

The Patriarchs

Blessed are You, Adonai our God, and the God of our fathers, God of Abraham, God of Isaac, and God of Jacob. The Great, Mighty, and Awe-inspiring God, the Most High God, Who bestows kindness and creates all, Who remembers the kindnesses of the fathers, and Who brings a Redeemer to their children's children for the sake of His Name with love. O King, Helper, Savior, and Shield. Blessed are You, Adonai, Shield of Abraham.

The Resurrection Power of God

You are forever mighty, my Lord, the Reviver of the Dead are You, great in salvation. He makes the wind blow and He makes the rain fall. He upholds the living in kindness, resurrects the dead with great mercy, supports the fallen, heals the sick, and is faithful with those who sleep in the dust. Who is like you, Master of Powerful Deeds, and who can compare to You, King, who causes death, and restores life, and makes Salvation sprout! And you are faithful to resurrect the dead. Blessed are You, Adonai, Resurrection of the Dead.

Holiness

You are Holy, and Your Name is Holy, and holy ones praise you every day for eternity, for You are God, the Great and Holy King. Blessed are You, Adonai, the Holy God.

Knowledge

You kindly give man the gift of knowledge, and teach wisdom to frail man. Give with grace from Yourself with wisdom, insight, and knowledge. Blessed are You, Adonai, the gracious Giver of Knowledge.

Repentance

Cause us to return, Our Father, to Your Torah, and draw us near, our King, to Your service, and cause us to return in perfect repentance before You. Blessed are You, Adonai, Who desires repentance.

Forgiveness

Forgive us, our Father, for we have made errors; pardon us, our King, for we have sinned willfully, for You are a Good and forgiving God. Blessed are You, Adonai, Gracious One, Who forgives abundantly.

Redemption

Notice, please, our affliction, take up our grievance, and quickly redeem us with a full redemption for the sake of Your Name, for You are God the Mighty Redeemer. Blessed are You, Adonai, Redeemer of Israel.

Health and Healing

Heal us, Adonai, and we will be healed, save us, and we will be saved, for You are our Praise. Bring cure and healing for all our sicknesses, sufferings, and ailments, for You are God and King, a faithful and compassionate Healer. Blessed are You, Adonai, Healer of the sick of His people Israel.

The Prosperous Year

Bless for us, Adonai our God, this year and all types of crops for good, and give dew and rain for blessing on the face of the earth, and satisfy us from its goodness, and bless our year like the best years for blessing. For You are the good and giving God Who blesses the years. Blessed are You, Adonai, Who blesses the years.

Ingathering of Exiles

Blow the great (trumpet) shofar for our freedom, raise the banner to gather our exiles and quickly gather us from the four corners of the earth to our Land. Blessed are You, Adonai, Who gathers in His scattered people Israel.

Restoration of Justice

Restore our judges as in former times, and our counselors as at the beginning. Remove from us sorrow and groaning, and soon reign over us, You, Adonai, only, with kindness and compassion, and justify us in righteousness and judgment. Blessed are You Adonai, the King Who loves righteousness and judgment.

The Righteous

Upon the righteous, upon the devout, upon the elders of the remnant of Your people the family of Israel, on the remnant of their scholars in houses of study, on the righteous converts and on us may Your compassion be aroused, please Adonai our God, and give a good reward to all who truly believe in Your Name. Make us to walk with them, and may we never feel ashamed, for in You we trust, and we depend upon Your great compassion. Blessed are You, Adonai, Supporter and Assurance of the Righteous.

Rebuilding Jerusalem

And to Jerusalem, Your city, may You return with compassion, and may You rest in it, as You have said. May You rebuild it speedily in our days as an eternal building, and may you speedily set up the throne of your servant David within it. Blessed are You, Adonai, Builder of Jerusalem.

Kingdom of the House of David

May the offspring of Your servant David soon flourish, and lift up his pride through Your salvation, for we hope for Your Salvation all day long. Blessed are You, Adonai, Who makes the pride of Salvation to flourish.

Acceptance of Prayer

Hear our voice, Adonai our God, have mercy and be compassionate to us, and accept our prayer with willingness and compassion, for you are God Who hears prayers and supplications. From before You, our King, turn us not away empty-handed. For You hear the prayer of Your people Israel with compassion. Blessed are You, Adonai, Who hears prayer.

Temple Service

Be favorable, Adonai, our God, toward Your people Israel and their prayer, and restore the service to the Holy of Holies of Your Temple. Accept the fire-offerings of Israel and their prayer with love and favor, and may the service of Your people Israel always be favorable to You. May our eyes behold Your returning to Zion in compassion. Blessed are You, Adonai, the Restorer of His Presence to Zion.

Thanksgiving

We thank You, for it is You Who are Adonai, the God of our
forefathers forever; the Rock of our lives, Shield of our
Salvation (Yeshua!) are You from generation to generation.
We will thank You and declare Your praise for our lives,
which are in your hands, our souls that are entrusted to You,
Your daily miracles, and for Your wonders and favors at all
times: evening, morning, and afternoon. The Good One, for
Your compassions were not exhausted, and the
Compassionate One, for Your kindnesses never ended; we
have always put our hope in You. For all these, may Your
Name be blessed and exalted, Our King, continually forever.
Everything alive will thank You, selah! And praise Your Name
in truth forever, for it is Good. O God of our salvation and
help, selah. The Good God. Blessed are You, Adonai, Your
Name is the Good One, and to You it is proper to give thanks.

Peace

Establish peace, goodness, blessing, life, graciousness, kind-
ness, and compassion upon us and upon all of Your people
Israel. Bless us Our Father, all of us together, with the light of
Your countenance, for with the light of Your countenance You
gave us, Adonai our God, the Torah of life and a love of kind-
ness, righteousness, blessing, compassion, life, and peace. And
may it be good in Your eyes to bless us and to bless all of Your
people Israel, in every season and in every hour with Your
peace. Blessed are You, Adonai, Who blesses His people Israel
with peace.

Conclusion
Insert Personal Supplications Here

My God, guard my tongue from evil and my lips from speaking deceit. To those who curse me, let my soul be silent, and let my soul be like dust to everyone. Open my heart to Your Torah, and then my soul will seek Your commandments. As for all those who plot evil against me, quickly nullify their counsel and disrupt their plans. May it be Your will, Adonai, my God and the God of my forefathers, that human jealousy may not rise against me, nor may I be jealous of others; may I not be angry today, and may I not anger You. Rescue me from the Evil Inclination, and place in my heart submissiveness and humility. O our King and our God, cause Your Name to be unified in Your world; rebuild Your city, lay the foundation of Your House, perfect Your Sanctuary; gather in the scattered exiles, redeem Your sheep, and make glad Your congregation. Act for Your Name's sake; act for Your right hand's sake, act for Your Torah's sake, act for Your sanctity's sake so that Your beloved ones may be given rest; let Your right hand save and respond to me. May the words of my mouth and the thoughts of my heart find graceful favor before You, Adonai, my Rock and my Redeemer.

He Who makes peace in His high places, may He make peace upon us, and upon all Israel. Amein.

May it be Your will, Adonai our God and the God of our forefathers, that the holy Temple be rebuilt speedily in our days. Grant us our portion in Your Torah, and may we serve You there with reverence as in ancient days and years. Then the descendants of Judah and Jerusalem will be pleasing to Adonai as in days of old and in former years.

GLOSSARY

Adonai—my Lord.

Alefbet—Hebrew alphabet

Am Ha-aretz—the "common people" in Yeshua's day; the Jewish religious elite looked down upon the am ha-aretz because they did not keep the oral traditions as scrupulously as did the Pharisees

Brit Chadashah—New Testament. In Hebrew, literally, "Renewed Covenant." The Hebrew word for new, chadash, also means renewed, as we apply the adjective to the New Moon. The moon is not new; it is the same moon. Its appearance is merely renewed to us each month. By the same token, Jeremiah 31:31 defines the terms of the New Covenant: the Torah will be written on the hearts of God's people. It is not a new Torah, but the old Torah renewed to us in a dynamic way because of the work of Yeshua, a better mediator than Moses.

Chok(im)—ordinances of the Torah which have no rational explanation; the only explanation is that "you are to be holy for I am holy."

Church Fathers—the leaders of the Christian Church after it shed its identity as a sect of Judaism. The teachings of the Church Fathers incorporated theologies and doctrines that taught against the goodness of the Torah as a manual for holy living, taught the Church has replaced Israel, and taught dispensationalism, all contrary to the Biblical pattern of progressive revelation. Each of these served to divide the Church from its Hebraic roots and eventually justified the Crusades, the Holocaust, The Inquisition, the pogroms, and slaughter and oppression of the Jews in Christian nations.

Gematria—the number value of a Hebrew letter, such as the "number of a man, 666." The value of 6 reflects the Hebrew letter vav, sixth letter of the alphabet. Each letter has a numerical value, significance, and the letters themselves are pictures.

El Shaddai—the Name of God revealed to Abraham that alludes to the nurturing attribute of God

Fathers of the World—the Jewish sages who compiled the Mishnah, Jewish oral law

Gemara—a rabbinic commentary on the Mishnah, Jewish oral law

Halakha—the way of walking and living out the commandments of Adonai in a practical way

Adonai—"The Name," often translated in all capital letters in English as LORD. It is the most sacred Name of God, and is wrongly translated as Jehovah.

Kanfot—a rectangular, four-cornered garment with fringes attached to each corner; it is worn by Jewish males

Kefa—Peter's Hebrew name.

Kippa—a Jewish skullcap, from the Hebrew root word for covering or atonement, *kippur*

Mashiach—Messiah; Christ

Menorah—a lampstand, specifically, the seven-branched golden lampstand that stood in the Holy Place of the Tabernacle and Temple

Minchah—an offering in the Temple made at 3:00 P.M.; also the 3:00 P.M. hour of prayer corresponding to the time of that offering

Mishnah—the Jewish oral law traditionally believed to have been passed down from Moses. Yeshua sometimes upheld the oral law and sometimes overruled it. His method of determining the validity of oral law was to judge whether it set aside a written commandment in favor of the traditions of men.

Mishpat(im)—judgments. The mishpatim often deal with ethical or moral laws.

Mitzvah—a commandment or a good deed

Rebbe/Rabbi—a Jewish spiritual leader or teacher

Ruach HaKodesh—Holy Spirit, or Holy Wind

Shaul—Paul's Hebrew name

Shema—"Hear O Israel; the LORD our God, the LORD is One." The greatest commandment

Shemoneh Esrei—eighteen, or the eighteen benedictions of the Amidah

Tallit—the Jewish prayer shawl worn over the clothes. It is rectangular, four-cornered garment with fringes affixed to the corners. Modern tallitot may be the traditional simple white woolen with black stripes, or may be decorative and woven or painted with bright colors and designs. The tallit worn by clergy in the synagogue may function as a vestment and be less functional than the traditional tallit, which also serves as the wedding canopy. Orthodox Jewish women do not wear a tallit, but it is common for Reform, Conservative, and Messianic Jewish women to wear feminine tallitot to synagogue.

Talmid(im)—disciple(s)

Talmud—the largest body of Jewish law and commentary containing the Mishnah, Gemara, and Tosefta

Tanakh—Old Testament. Tanakh is an acronym for Torah, Neviim, Ketuvim, or Law, Prophets, and Writings, the ancient divisions of the Hebrew Bible. The books of the Tanakh are the same as, but are not arranged in the same order as Christian Bibles.

Torah—the first five books of the Bible, misunderstood as "law" in English translations. The Torah is more accurately God's teaching and instruction. It contains topics such as science, history, priestly procedures, civil statutes, ordinances, health, agriculture, commandments, prophecies, prayer, animal husbandry, architecture, civics, and many others. The root word of Torah comes from the Hebrew word *yarah*, which means "to hit the mark." Torah may also be used to refer to all of the Hebrew Bible, or even to its smallest meaning, a procedure. Torah may be used by Messianic Jews to refer to the entire Bible from Genesis to Revelation, for the Torah is the foundation for all the Scriptures. The Prophets point Israel back to the Torah. The Psalms teach one to love the Torah as King David loved it. The Writings teach the consequences of departing from the Torah and the rewards for returning to it. The New Testament brings the Torah to its fullest meaning in the person Yeshua the Messiah, and much of the New Testament quotes the Tanakh.

Yerushalayim—Jerusalem

Yeshua—Jesus' Hebrew name; salvation

RESOURCES TO DIG DEEPER

Liturgical Resources:
Messianic Shabbat Siddur compiled by Jeremiah Greenberg
First Steps in Hebrew Prayer by Dr. Danny ben Gigi

Church History:
Our Hands are Stained with Blood by Michael L. Brown
The Church and the Jews by Dan Gruber
Too Long in the Sun by Richard Rives
Yeshua: a Guide to the Real Jesus and the Original Church by Dr. Ronald Moseley

Hebraic Roots:
Torah Rediscovered; Take Hold by Ariel and D'vorah Berkowitz
Paul, the Jewish Theologian by Brad Young
Seven Festivals of the Messiah by Eddie Chumney
The Complete Jewish Bible translated by Dr. David Stern

Messianic TV:
www.israelnet.tv

Educational Institutions/Torah Studies:
American Institute of Holy Land Studies, Sherwood, Arkansas; www.aihls.org
First Fruits of Zion/www.ffoz.org
www.torahresource.com

Hebrew Instruction:
www.hebrewworld.com
www.easyhebrew.com

Messianic Jewish Products and Books:
1-800-4YESHUA
www.messianicjewish.net

Israeli History and Balanced Political Research:
From Time Immemorial by Joan Peters
www.honestreporting.com

Standing With Israel
Order Form

Postal orders: The Olive Branch
PO Box 1140
London, KY 40743

E-mail orders: www.standingwithisrael.com

Please send *Standing With Israel* to:

Name: _____

Address: _____

City: _____   State: _____

Zip: _____   Telephone: (_____) _____

Book Price: $14.95

Shipping: $3.00 for the first book and $1.00 for each additional book to cover shipping and handling within US, Canada, and Mexico. International orders add $6.00 for the first book and $2.00 for each additional book.

Or order from:
ACW Press
1200 HWY 231 South #273
Ozark, AL 36360

(800) 931-BOOK

or contact your local bookstore